Seeker at Cassandra Marsh

Seeker at Cassandra Marsh

Olive M. Anderson

CHRISTIAN HERALD BOOKS
Chappaqua, New York

Library of Congress Cataloging in Publication Data

Anderson, Olive M., 1915-
SEEKER AT CASSANDRA MARSH
   1. Natural history—Michigan. 2. Natural history—Great Lakes region. I. Title.
II. Title: Cassandra Marsh
QH105.M5A73   500.9774   78-56976
ISBN 0-915684-41-1

Artwork was done by Nels Anderson.

FIRST EDITION

CHRISTIAN HERALD BOOKS, 40 OVERLOOK DRIVE, CHAPPAQUA, NEW YORK 1(

Printed in the United States of America

For my parents,
Francis John and Olive Angeline Aucock

TABLE OF CONTENTS

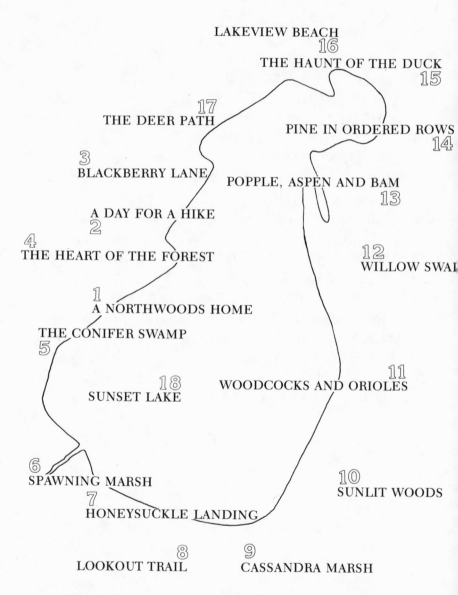

LAKEVIEW BEACH
16

THE HAUNT OF THE DUCK
15

17
THE DEER PATH

PINE IN ORDERED ROWS
14

3
BLACKBERRY LANE

POPPLE, ASPEN AND BAM
13

A DAY FOR A HIKE
2

4
THE HEART OF THE FOREST

12
WILLOW SWAI

1
A NORTHWOODS HOME

THE CONIFER SWAMP
5

11
18
SUNSET LAKE

WOODCOCKS AND ORIOLES

6
SPAWNING MARSH

10
SUNLIT WOODS

7
HONEYSUCKLE LANDING

8
LOOKOUT TRAIL

9
CASSANDRA MARSH

The numbers and titles on the above map correspond to the chapters of the book.

A Northwoods Home

I was sitting in the firecircle outside our cabin cleaning blueberries. A chipmunk darted playfully about my feet, scampered toward the cabin when I tossed out a handful of discarded berries, then watched with bright wary eyes from a hole beneath the doorstep.

Crackling sounds came from the lakeside woods. Someone must be coming along the path through the birches. I looked up expectantly. The sounds increased, punctuated by several sharp retorts. Through white birch trunks I saw a large dark tree slant toward the lake.

I heard a gigantic whoosh ... thud ... splash ... washing waves, then silence. I jumped to my feet, scattering berries. For an amazed moment I stood with the pan in my hand, then remembered to set it down before I dashed down the winding path to the lake.

One of the twin white pines was prostrate in the shallow water of the beach, pointing straight out into the lake. The two tall trees, leaning slightly out over the water, had long served us as a landmark.

I turned and ran back up the path calling, "Fred! Fred!" before I remembered that my husband was sleeping. He'd arrived late the night before from a non-stop drive to get back to our Michigan cabin after a Canadian fishing trip. He appeared at the screen door looking sleepy and alarmed.

"Did you hear it?" I asked.

"Hear what?" he mumbled. He was used to my excitement over a strange bird, a new plant.

"The pine fell. . . ."

"Pine . . . what pine?"

"One of the twin lakefront ones! Just now. I saw it!" I said, my breath coming in painful bursts.

Fred started out the door, then looked down at his bare feet. "I'll get my shoes." He caught up with me at the lakefront.

We inspected the surviving tree. The two pines had grown with their branches intertwined, but the remaining one seemed only to have bright patches of skinned bark. We could see no other damage.

"What do you suppose happened?" I asked.

"Hasn't stormed lately, has it?" Fred asked in answer.

"Not since I've been here. Plenty of rain, but no wind. But both pines were hit by lightning a couple of years ago, remember? We saw the raw furrow running back and forth from one tree to another when we were out on the lake at fishing time."

"Just scratches. The lightning only gouged out a thin line of bark."

"There isn't a strong wind today, just a normal northwoods breeze. Do you suppose the roots were weakened here at the edge of the bank when the lake was high?"

We walked through bunchberries, blueberries, lily of the valley and bracken and found the six-foot stub, with its splintered top of raw yellow wood. The roots were still strongly intertwined with those of the other pine.

I walked up to the stump expecting to see a rotted hollow. The wood looked healthy, with only dark stains at the center. I sniffed. There was a strong odor which was familiar to me, the acrid odor of fungi about their destructive work.

"Smell this," I said to Fred. "Fungus weakened the wood fibers until the trunk wasn't strong enough to support the weight of the tree, curving out over the lake the way it did."

10

Fred started off through the woods. "Where are you going?" I called.

"To get Bob," Fred answered. He was back in a few minutes with our neighbor.

"A generous supply of good white pine for starting fires there, my friends," Bob declared, shaking out his pipe in his deliberate, dignified fashion. "I'll bring my chain saw over and we'll cut it up before you can say 'northwoods sourdough pancakes.'"

"Should make quite a woodpile. You can take a share for your fireplace," Fred said.

"Is that all you see, firewood?" I asked indignantly. A big blue heron had flapped to an awkward perch in the very top of this tree one night as we came in from fishing. Another evening I'd sat on the beach beneath it, head tipped back to watch the red squirrel feasting on the green pinecones that filled the top of the trees every other year. I remembered combing fragments of scales from my hair later, part of the debris that showered down as the chickaree expertly harvested the seeds.

I looked at the fallen giant. Its long-needled green branches stretched far out into the lake. The ones on the upper side still reached up gracefully to the sky; those underneath were crushed and broken.

A memorial service, with mourners and eulogies would be more fitting than a sawing bee. I kept my thoughts to myself as I saw the men's indulgent smiles. I would never get over the pain of the fallen tree, whether it was so by accident or design. Fred had to cut one of the white birches near the cabin doorstep when it developed a fungus shelf, because it leaned dangerously over the cabin. Four walls of hemlock siding nailed to a two-by-four frame and painted to blend into the birches, plus a green-shingled roof—that was our cabin.

A bracket on a handsome birch near our picture window

went undetected, and Bob discovered the tree broken over our rooftree after a winter storm. Luckily, it had not broken through our handmade structure, so the interior of the cabin had not been left open to weather and animal-life as it might have been.

"By the way, Olive," Bob broke into my reveries. "I have some lengthy errands in town today. Would you look in on my dear Cora occasionally while I am gone?"

"Of course. I'll be glad to," I replied as he moved off. Age was confusing his wife's fine mind, making her steps uncertain.

"See you tomorrow, my friends," Bob called in the distance.

Fred finished his piece of blueberry pie that evening, and pushed back his canvas captain's chair to enjoy his coffee. "I'll catch some bluegills to go with the rest of the pie tomorrow," he said.

I smiled to myself, relieved at any sign that catching the "big ones" in Canada had not completely spoiled fishing in this area for him. Keeper-sized pike are now scarce in our own lake. I missed our evening fishing. True, I didn't often go with my husband in recent years, but it was companionable to know he was fishing the lake when I hiked of an evening, and could push through shrubs to the lakefront and check on his luck in the pike hole once in a while.

Joining him in the boat on rare occasions now brought back memories of our early days in the woods, when evening fishing was a nightly experience. Then Fred had eagerly fished, providing both recreation and food, while I absorbed the peacefulness of lake and sky and tree-lined shoreline, with pencil and notebook handy to record my impressions.

"Maybe I'll hike around the lake," I said in answer to his plans for tomorrow. I had increasingly been drawn to the woods, with an insatiable curiosity that led to long hours of

12

exploring and examining specimens, and even longer hours with books, learning about what I had seen and heard.

Fred yawned. "I'm ready for bed again."

"Didn't you rest at all on the trip?"

"Just stretched out in the back of the station wagon while one of the other men drove. That's the only way you can get from northern Manitoba to Illinois in twenty-five hours."

"You should have rested at home after you got the fish safely in our freezer."

"Well, you know how it is. . . ," he said. "The telephone would have started ringing."

Yes. I knew how it was. This cabin we'd built with our own hands in the middle of Hiawatha National Forest had been a retreat for us both.

"We'd get bored, vacationing at the same place year after year. We want to see something new," friends had told us. But here in this clearing in the forest, under a shaded roof repeating the colors of the forest trees above it, Fred and I found the feeling of belonging.

"You make any place we live look like home," Fred had told me when we were first married. Those places numbered into the dozens by now, and although the parsonages we lived in had looked like home, we always knew that another congregation, another new home, lay in the future. As I had chosen colors for walls and hung pictures, I was aware of trustees, parsonage committees and the people who would live there after me.

This cabin with its rough board walls and rustic furnishings had become, in the twenty years we had vacationed here, the most permanent part of our itinerant lives. Thumbtacked to its walls are children's crayon drawings, brown and curling at the edges, a "poetic" tribute to fisherman Fred, presented at a ceremonial campfire on the beach by guests he taught to fish, and a "Happy Birthday" plate from a surprise premature

13

birthday party for our own grandchildren. We had had to use thumbtacks because nails were apt to protrude through to the outside.

A smooth round stone from the gravel pit where we saw a bear keeps the current fishing regulations in place on the clock shelf. The shelf is a scrap of four-inch-wide wood nailed between the studding, to hold the cheap alarm clock that we sometimes remember to wind. Above it is a collection of the inevitable fisherman's prayers, old woodgathering permits and boat licenses, a crude sketch on a scrap of yellow paper giving directions to the cranberry bog.

On the rare occasions when I sweep the crannies of the exposed two-by-four studding around the edge of the wood floor, my broom dislodges a piece of smooth dark wood my daughter and I brought back with us from the next lake the day we lost our way in the swamp. I always tuck it back into its corner.

The pine boards nailed together across the end of the cabin to make bookshelves are weighed down with a clutter of memories. A scene cut from a magazine is propped there, framed in sculptured cardboard by our son the year he spent so much time at the desk-table he'd made of pine boards, experimenting with craft ideas learned in his first art class at college.

The mantle behind the wood stove holds a heap of natural objects in front of a dried mahogany bracket I identified as *Polyporus tsugae*, found on a hemlock log that has long since rotted away. The dusty, lichened nest tied to the crotch of maple twigs with a shred of birch bark swung next to our bedroom window one spring until the pair of red-eyed vireos abandoned it. They evidently didn't appreciate the light which streamed from the curtainless window until all hours of the night as we indulged our bedtime reading habits to the full.

A pile of tattered comic books, most of which had long since

14

lost their covers, fill one corner of the shelves, accumulated by two generations of children. They had been used for many purposes by many people. They keep children quiet when grown-ups want to talk, provide entertainment for visiting youngsters who don't know what to do in the woods, make rainy days bearable.

Most recently the comics gave me an up-to-date weather report. I was immersed in work at my desk, oblivious to all else, when I heard a tap at my door. "We've come for the comic books," the neighbor children announced happily. I looked out the window. Sure enough, raindrops ran down the pane, and others were dripping down from one leaf to another in the trees outside my window, each leaf shaking in its turn. I had promised to loan the children comic books on the first rainy day.

The shelf above the comics holds a record of family excursions in the area. Some of the bright folders are reminders of pleasant days of sightseeing, some of hopes unfulfilled. More than one of them advertises places and events long since become history. When guests thumb through them and decide they want to take the boat ride to Grand Island and eat dinner at the hotel there, we have to tell them neither is possible, nor has been for a good many years. It is something we'd always intended to do, and at the last minute decided we'd rather stay in the woods *this* year. And the years ran out. Telling our guests that the lumber for our cabin was cut on Grand Island is a poor substitute, but it pleases us.

Our ties to this place are pleasant ones, but they are threatened. We had built the cabin with my sister's family and shared ownership and use with them. Children married and added more families. Retirement time was close for Fred, and with increased use this small structure couldn't meet everyone's needs.

The cabin lot was leased from the Forest Service, and recreational use of the area between Lake Michigan and Lake Superior boomed after the opening of the Mackinac Bridge. Government policy might do away with the leased-lot privilege in favor of campsites.

I looked forward to more time, to leisurely summer months in the woods when Fred no longer had the responsibility of a church. I knew he'd not be happy without preaching once in a while, but those times could be scheduled as he wished. This dream of mine was threatened by my husband's increasing lack of interest in his part of the northwoods, now that Canadian fishing had priority.

"This may be the most permanent setting for my life, but I'd better not depend upon it," I thought, as I washed dishes at the small kitchen sink, looking out the window at the late sunlight glowing on white birch trunks, sparkling on blue lake.

But the day was not yet over. Bob tapped on the window where Fred sat reading. "Did Cora come this way?" he asked. "I can't find her since I had to force her to take her medicine."

"We haven't seen her," Fred said, "but she may have gone down the road. I'll check."

"Thank you, my good friend," Bob said. "I'll go the other direction."

It would be dark before long. Increasingly Cora wandered off, sometimes looking for friends who used to live in neighboring cabins, sometimes in rebellion, reacting as a child when Bob had to insist on matters concerning her own health and safety.

Though we all shared the concern and the search when this happened, it was usually Bob who found her. And so it was that evening. When Fred returned alone, we both walked toward the log cabin next door. Bob and Cora were just coming into their clearing.

"She . . . wasn't there. The door was . . . you know. . . ." Cora gestured vaguely as we met them. "I pushed. . . ," she struggled painfully for the word.

"The door was locked?" I suggested. Her face lit up for a

16

moment, when I supplied the correct words, then clouded again.

"I looked in the window. . . ." She demonstrated with hands on either side of her eyes. "She . . . you know . . . boy . . . girl . . . build . . . that woman . . . she wasn't there. She invited me to lunch. . . ." Cora's words trailed off into meaninglessness.

"Cora was looking for Agnes," Bob said to us. Then turning to Cora, he tried to explain. "She isn't there, dear, don't you remember? Her daughter and family were at the cabin last week." Gradually he urged her toward their cabin door. Fred and I followed the wooded path through the forest to our cabin, stumbling over protruding roots in the darkening woods.

"That woman," Cora had called her friend. The two families built their cabins here, the first on the lake, and worked and visited together year after year. Now she could not say her friend's name. Cora had turned to me in her own cabin this afternoon and pointed to Bob when he returned, saying, "What is that man doing here?"

Yes, change came not only to the forest, but to its inhabitants. Cora's rich, cultured voice was the same as when she had served on university staffs, been part of the social life of the nation's capital. I had once laughed at the incongruity of a pair of long white gloves I found under a chair, in the rustic log cabin she had helped chink. The articulate, sophisticated Cora was now a mindless child stammering for words.

The friends who had shared the earliest years with them came to the woods rarely now because severe illness had struck them immediately after their retirement. The cabin next to theirs was usually boarded and silent. We had fed its owners blueberry pancakes one morning and seen them off to their home in the Lower Peninsula. Two weeks later the husband had died of a heart attack.

Illinois friends had built the cabin on the other side of us, the fourth of our west cove neighbors, but they decided they preferred the mobility of a house trailer. Of the two families who bought that cabin from them, death in one and illness in the other brought ownership of the cabin full circle. Young friends of ours with a family now vacation next door, fish and pick berries with us. Their children help ease the distance we live from our own grandchildren several states away.

The accumulation of thoughts about change in this one day swept over me with devastating effect. Is nothing ever the same from one day to the next?

> Why, Lord, why?
> A small word, a large question,
> Echoing down the ages.
> Why can't my world stay as it is?
> I cherish the furnishings of my life.
> They are comfortable, familiar—mine.
>
> Yes, Lord, I know.
> I have glibly assured others
> Stricken by the storms of change.
> But this is my life, my woods,
> My neighbors, my cabin, my family.
>
> The word "my" must reach you
> As often as "why." Forgive me.
> Countless times have I given you
> My world, my life. They are yours.
> You have given them to me.
> I return them to you
> With praise and thanksgiving.
>
> There. Again I've vanquished the "my."
> Still, if I am honest,
> I must confess to a lingering echo,
> "Why must there be change? Why?"

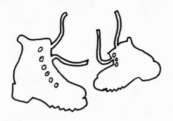

A Day For A Hike

I visited the fallen pine first thing the next morning, stepping quickly up onto the roots of the cluster of trees that leaned out over the lake as waves from a passing boat invaded my shoes. Our beach this year was a foot of wet sand. How many times I had stood in the shelter of these trees that twined roots, trunk and branches together. The three cedars, a maple and a birch made a sheltered spot for our boat landing.

Several yards to my left a dead pine, still firmly rooted in the bank, reached out horizontally over the water. The trunk was partially immersed, its tip curved gracefully skyward with a ragged remnant of branches. I had sometimes used it in the foreground of sunset pictures.

To my right, past the fallen pine, another dead snag reached out over the lake. It protruded from the group of green cedars which marked the approximate boundary line between our lot and Bob and Cora's.

I remembered the morning I wakened early and sat on the beach wrapped in a blanket. Mist swirled over the lake as I listened to the forest come awake. Ducks talked to each other somewhere in that mist. A crow flew cawing over the forest on an early errand. I heard a watery "plop" nearby and saw a kingfisher return to his perch on the pine snag. He could see the smallest minnow move in the clear shallow water beneath the tree.

In the silence after the splash, I heard the merest whisper of a scrabbling sound on the bark of the dock trees beside me. Too quiet for a red squirrel, or even a chipmunk. Then my eyes caught a shadowy motion on the horizontal cedar trunk. A dainty mouse picked its way furtively along and disappeared. I got up quietly, clutching my blanket to keep it from trailing in the sand. At eye level there was a hole where a branch had broken off, making a snug home for the mouse.

A loud splash sounded on my right. The kingfisher was using the dead cedar for his diving perch now. He flew from one snag to the other, following the school of minnows.

"That's the kingfisher's perch!" I objected later when Bob said he'd knock that snag off next time he had his saw out.

And yet, I thought now, I'd spent one whole day with a hand axe, grubbing out the sweet gale bushes that grew where I wanted to set my beach chair. That was in our early years at the cabin. I only knew that the shrubs had a tough, stubborn root and a pungent, pleasing odor as I hacked away, doing a thorough job of it. I had made a few feet of sandy beach for years when the lake was high.

Leatherleaf bushes, also called Cassandra, grew just beyond the sweet gale. They are very similar, except that leatherleafs are sturdier in appearance. I am not sure I could have won a battle with them.

Only as I became more curious and observing did I realize that I had destroyed wild shrubs with a lovely name as well as a pleasing fragrance. True, there were still thriving thickets of the sweet gale, but they made no attempt to reclaim the spot I had cleared. Since I had removed the roots, too, the sand remained bare.

I had made a permanent break in the continuous cover along the bank. This is where we had watched the mink play in early years. It had been a long time since we'd had to mink-proof our bait box. Our presence alone discouraged wildlife, but had I, by making a change in the forest, also destroyed a part of the habitat of the mink? The fallen pine, the dead snags, were natural ones. What happens when man gets into the act, too?

20

I looked uneasily at the small square of sand. Yet we had all enjoyed landing here instead of pulling the prow of the boat up into the scratchy bushes and jumping for the bank. And how often through the years this spot had been my secluded meditating nook.

My eyes rested on the fallen pine, then swept around the lake before me. I couldn't locate the dead stub that used to protude above the treeline at the end of the lake, where fishermen often saw an eagle fishing early in the morning. Had a storm destroyed it? What other changes had there been since we'd known these woods? I would use my hike around the lake today to consider them, along with the nagging "why?" about change in my own life.

The weather sounded promising. Not that I hadn't hiked in all kinds of weather—with raincoat handy, bundled in shapeless layers of warm clothing against a brisk fall wind, or in a long-sleeved cotton shirt that was too warm but necessary in the summer for protection against mosquitoes.

But I had better do a bit of housekeeping first. I remembered that Fred's gear was still strewn about the cabin in duffle bags. So I took a last look at the lake and started up the tree-shaded path to the cabin.

Was that a bright fungus pushing up through the dead leaves over there or just a wintergreen berry? I left the path to investigate. It was a wintergreen berry, plump, waxy and scarlet. As usual this time of year, a white bell-like bloom with a faint blush of pink was beside it. It hung under the evergreen waxed leather leaves two inches from the forest floor. On a nearby wintergreen plant green berries were developing.

This was where one of the chipmunks always headed when his pouches were full of the popcorn we put out for him. I had always been going to locate the entrance to his burrow. Was it under that big old hemlock stump? It would take a lot of searching and patient watching. Finding a fresh heap of dirt was no help, because the clever striped creatures begin their

21

home at the back door, take dirt out that way, then seal it tight. Sometime I would spend a day looking for his carefully hidden front door.

I hadn't begun to exhaust the wonders of our own cabin lot! As I flew up the path to tackle the household chores, I remembered that the pipsissewa was in bloom halfway between the cabin and the lake. One year I had discovered the glossy, dark green leaves and green buds in June. Since then I had often seen the dried seed pods in August, but this year I was here to see them bloom. The clusters of precise pink flowers were displayed on erect stems with graceful curves at the blossom end. They had been worth waiting for.

I laughed contentedly to myself as I swept the cabin doorstep, sorry for the people who had to go new places to see new things.

> Your marvels are never ending, Lord,
> Your ways past finding out,
> Your wonders beyond man to fathom,
> Your mind altogether unlike our own.
>
> The mystery of life is yours alone,
> The scale of it beyond our imagining.
> We probe here and there,
> Split an atom,
> Aghast at the reverberations,
> Circle the earth
> And leap upon the surface of the moon.
>
> And still . . .
> Out there is the universe,
> On whose threshold we've scarce
> Set one trembling foot,
> Peering beyond into the dark . . .
> The unknown.

And all the while
There are mysteries at my own doorstep.
Thank you, Lord, that this is so.
You would not be God
If I could fully understand
You and your creation.

"You're taking your lunch? Just to walk around the lake?"
Fred asked. I didn't tell him I usually took most of a day at it
when I was here alone or with guests. This was another of the
changes. As Fred's interest in fishing the lake waned, I sometimes came to the cabin alone or with friends who enjoyed
exploring the northwoods with me.

"I do a lot besides walk," I said, chuckling. "How many
sandwiches do you want in your lunch, and do you want milk or
tea in your thermos?"

"Just put in plenty of everything. Blue Joe Lake is a long way
from anywhere. Will you give me a hand with the boat when
you get through there?"

"Who's going with you?" I asked, knowing my husband was
not a solitary fisherman.

"Some boys are visiting in a cabin down the lake. I'll take
them where, hopefully, they can catch some pan fish."

I waved Fred down the lane and watched him back the car
safely around the stumps and trees, onto the service road. The
aluminum boat strapped to the top of the car seemed to float
along by itself through the forest. Then it, too, disappeared.

Yes, this was a day to take my camera and my whole supply of
film along, I confirmed as I turned toward the lake. It was going
to be one of the blue and green forest days, blue of sky and lake,
green of the forest, with accents of white fleecy clouds. Cool
enough so far for a light jacket. I would need the pockets
anyway for storage.

No one vacationing on the lake could take as long as I to walk around it. Not many would see any reason even to start. Except, of course, the year the lake was so low that there was a wide sandy beach completely surrounding it. Then the beach could be walked in less than an hour without ever detouring, and circling the lake became a popular activity.

There is really nothing to make anyone suspect what he is missing. Our lake is three-fourths of a mile long by half a mile wide, not large enough for high powered boats and the water-skiing most vacationers want. The lake is so ordinary looking, rimmed with a green border that varies only in height and shades of color. One of our windows at home was draped with fabric that had been recut to fit a half dozen parsonage windows through the years. The northwoods scene on the fabric, a photographic print, might be our lake. I hoped the drapes would last to curtain a retirement home window.

The first year Fred fished in Canada, I went along for the adventure, half fearful it would spoil my joy in our own woods and lake. We traveled forty-five miles by open boat, through various waterways and lakes of the far north, to reach our remote camp. The small bay on which the camp is located is larger than our own Michigan lake.

I was confined for a week on a rock-bound shore that glaciers had scoured clean, while Fred and his companions fished faraway bays. It is a land of lichens, stunted spruce trees clinging to bare rock and hardy shrubs covering boulders. The bush country on all sides is monotonous in its sameness, and I had not dared to wander out into the trackless expanses.

I wouldn't have missed the experience for anything, especially the loon chorus on the moonlight night. I liked to think that the pair of loons that used to entertain us on our own lake in early years had joined it. When we returned to our own cabin in Hiawatha Forest, I had a new appreciation of its endless variety of habitats and new wonders to discover. I could freely hike and explore with familiar landmarks to keep me oriented.

The small sandy basin which contains our lake, like dozens of others in the area, was formed by the glaciers that scoured the Canadian Shield. In their advances and retreats they eventually left the Great Lakes in their present forms. The sand we live on had been the bed of a post-glacial great lake, and before that was likely once part of the Canadian rock. Living on the far boundary of the glacier, we gained what the glacier-scoured country had lost.

"I'd better empty my shoes of any Canadian remnants before I start hiking," I thought to myself, smiling as I sat on a firecircle log to untie my sturdy walking shoes. A chipmunk peered hopefully from beneath the doorstep. "No food for you this time," I told him.

I collected my gear, checking off items from the list I'd fastened inside the top of my camera bag. Camera, film, binoculars, hand lens, foil for reflector. Raincoat, plastic square for close-up photography in wet places. Kleenex, mosquito dope, notebook and pencil, nature guides. Folded paper bags for specimens.

Oh. Better leave room for lunch. A compact one. A sandwich generously filled with meat, an apple and a handful of cookies for noontime. Candy bar and extra apple for energy snacks, hard fruit candies for thirst, raisins in a pocket to nibble as I walked. That should do it.

With everything neatly packed in pockets in the camera bag slung over my shoulder or in the red hiking bag carried in my hand, I was ready. The bag could be set down when I needed my hands free for camera or binoculars, or hung over my arm if there was no convenient spot to set it.

Where was my hiking hat? There. On the nail behind the door. It would keep my head protected from direct sun when I walked in the open and from twigs and branches that would snag my hair as I pushed through thickets.

I pulled the rough handmade door shut behind me. Breakfast dishes were hidden under the sink. There'd be plenty of time for them after the sun went down.

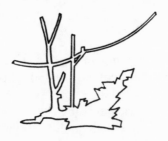

Blackberry Lane

A sense of urgency filled me. When I was alone at the cabin I usually let the neighbors know where I was going, but today Fred knew, and this was a morning for communing with nature, not neighbors.

I walked briskly down the lane. If I was looking for change in this forest I loved, I might as well start with the drastic ones right at hand, within sight of the cabin.

When we built twenty years ago, there were only two other cabins on the lake and we looked down our lane into dense hardwood forest. Beyond the service road that paralleled the lake, there were no birches to lighten the woods, as at the lakefront. The canopy of mature maple, beech and hemlock discouraged sunlight, and consequently other growth. Whip-poorwills and owls serenaded us at the very boundary of our lot. We used to step immediately into the forest.

Now I could look ahead and see sunlight flooding the area. A few years after we had built our cabin a swath of trees bordering the service road was cut to make way for a power line through the woods. Cabins on our lake had access to electricity, and the line ran through the forest, across the swamps, to the resort and cabin area on the next lake. Civilization had made its first inroads into our wilderness, even though we did not indulge in its benefits. We were here to rough it, and I resented the intrusion.

A bird was singing in the top of a slender towering maple. I whipped out my binoculars, my foot slipping in the mud as I did so. I caught my balance without moving my eyes from the treetop. As usual, I saw nothing but leaves. A mature forest is a discouraging place to birdwatch in the middle of the summer, and I am not much good at it anyway with my near-sighted eyes. Besides, it is difficult to watch birds and mushrooms at the same time!

I slipped the binocular strap around my neck and looked at my muddy shoes. That was one thing that hadn't changed—the mudhole at the end of our lane. No one ever really gets stuck in it, since it has a sandy bottom, but it can slide a car into a tree or stump.

The whole service road was greasy looking in this rainy summer. Maple seedlings hung over it, shutting out any sun that might get through the treetops, brushing the car on both sides as we drove through. Today the road was a green, mud-floored tunnel through the woods.

I used the road for hiking when I wanted fast access to a favorite haunt, usually to catch the light at the right angle for a picture. Today I wanted to take a good look at the clearing under the power line. I would use it as my route to the west end of the lake.

First I needed to cross the strip of forest left between the road and the power line. It is only a few yards wide and didn't seem to have changed much. The floor was still nearly bare, a carpet of dun-colored flattened leaves with partridgeberry or an occasional bit of moss poking through. It was impossible to walk straight across it though. I picked my way over and around moldering logs and fallen branches, and climbed up and down the humps and hollows they caused.

Cautiously I pushed through a barrier of blackberry canes and stepped out into a sunlit corridor through the woods, with poles and power line traveling down the middle of it.

Years ago, when the line went through, I was not as curious as now. I knew that someone had contracted to cut the trees and remove the wood of commercial value. I also remembered that Fred salvaged a black cherry log which was left behind. The log eventually became a handsome pair of cherry end tables for our parsonage living rooms, a constant reminder of the northwoods no matter where we lived.

A year after the cutting, the abandoned logs and stumps were covered with twining masses of false buckwheat vines. I thought they were wild morning glories until one day I caught my foot in a tangle of them and found they had tiny spikes of inconspicuous blossoms that weren't at all like morning glory blossoms.

I have two vivid recollections of that period. The first is of brushing away clouds of mosquitoes as I pushed aside the damp masses of vines to photograph mushrooms. White, purple, gray and bright orange fungi had miraculously appeared on the decomposing wood lying all around me.

I was so enthralled that I was oblivious to the insects that lit again on my hands and wrists as I held the camera, and on my ankles and face as I sprawled in the awkward positions needed to photograph growths on the underside of logs.

Untangling arms and legs after snapping the shutter was no easy job. I sometimes discovered a sharp pain in my side where a stick had pressed, or a skinned ankle. That night when all the bites started itching at once, I regretted not taking the time out for mosquito-proofing. But that evening, studying my books, I had identified the bright orange brackets as *Polyporous cinnabarinus* and those woody purple balls as *Daldinia concentrica*. And I had pictures to prove it!

My other memory is from October of the same year. I had coaxed a friend, who had come to the woods with us for leisure, solitude and reading while her husband fished, to leave the warm fire long enough to go for a walk with me. The buckwheat vines were a lovely wine shade, and bright fall leaves had drifted in from the bordering trees.

I began poking around the stumps, finding colorful mushroom arrangements to photograph. Bette obligingly pulled vines, too, and then began finding strange objects on her own. Soon she was exclaiming, "Olive, what's this? And what are those black things? Are they mushrooms?" Between Bette's finds and my own, my camera was busy. It was impossible to get them all.

Bette watched my antics for a while, then asked in a puzzled way, "Why do you photograph some and not others? Do you have a reason? You didn't pay any attention to the beautiful pink cap I found in the moss, but you spent a long time photographing those horrible-looking black fingers poking up around the stump."

That was the question which had fixed the scene in my memory. I had found it difficult to answer. The glib reply was, "I already have good pictures of some." This was partly true, but I realized it played only a small part in my thinking. Why are some things more intriguing to me than others?

The human mind is a marvelous contraption, and each person is unique. Many friends had walked these woods with me. Some even circled the lake. Harry and Betty (not the Bette of the last paragraphs) saw birds everywhere, even in October. The slightest chirp or fleetingest motion caught their attention. Gladys saw frogs and moths. Rita saw birds and was as captivated by everything in the northwoods as I. Anna, my first hiking companion, looked closely at the most commonplace natural object and marveled at what she saw through a hand lens. Anna didn't need a forest. One stump was a world of wonder to her. Or one leaf. Fred has an excellent eye for eagles, ducks or herons, since they are all fellow fishers.

To all appearances, I was starting off on my lake jaunt today by myself. But I wasn't alone. These companions were all with me, enriching my memories, expanding my interests, opening my eyes.

And always there is the Creator of it all.

> Alone? Another inept word.
> I am surrounded by creation,
> Knowing full well
> The Creator is in all he creates,
> Even me,
> Who in my smugness
> Forgets.
> Forgive me, Lord,
> It is when I am alone
> That I become most aware of you.
> You are my aloneness.
> Walk in my stride,
> Breathe with my breath,
> Be the warmth of the sunshine,
> The cool of the breeze,
> The scratch of the briar,
> The caress of leaves.
> Be my awareness.

Other vegetation had sprung up under the power line. Bracken took hold out here in the open, and seedlings of all kinds began to form a story above the trailing vines. To my eyes, not too observing then, it was a mass of new green growth. I could still easily push through it to find the stump that was apt to have the fragile "apple blossom" clusters of fungus or the one with dainty clusters of long-stemmed Mycena. I knew which log would have the largest variety of fungus growth upon it, where the mycelium of the fungus had completely invaded, but not yet used up the nutrients needed to fruit. October is the peak month for wood-growing fungi, and I made the most of the two or three days in the woods that

Fred and I sometimes managed to steal then from a busy schedule.

In the spring I checked to see the new woody brackets that had appeared, and could sometimes find remnants from seasons I had missed. One spring I arrived to find my hunting grounds ruined.

The mature woods back of us had undergone a selective cutting operation during the winter, a regular Forest Service practice. The contract had been let to a local timber outfit, and included the building of an access road across the swamp that was between us and the highway, and on down the power line clearing.

My mushroom logs and stumps had been piled and burned, or bulldozed to the edge of the woods. In early spring the ground was a barren, machine-trampled mess, with two muddy ruts running the length of the clearing. It had been used to get machinery and men in and logs out.

The ground wasn't bare long. When the growing season arrived, I was in the woods again. I found tall plants of pale pink and yellow corydalis blooming in the tire tracks, in a clearing, just as the flower book said. In the green that clothed the opening again I found the familiar Indian cucumber root and bristly sarsaparilla. Sturdy bracken reappeared and tiny berry seedlings were everywhere. Each season something new dominated the growth and caught my attention.

Residents used pickup trucks from time to time to remove firewood from the slash left after the lumbering operation, so a road wide enough for a car was kept open through the clearing.

Raspberry bushes at the edge of this track matured enough to bear a few berries that I lunched on as I passed by. One year I had hurried back to the cabin for a pail. The crop was abundant, and had ripened just at the time of our August vacation. We had fresh raspberry pies along with the usual blueberry ones, and raspberry jam to take home with us.

The next year I found only a few scattered berries. Long, lavender blackberry canes reached out to snag my jacket as I peered under them. The sturdy canes, as big around as my thumb, were taller than my head, and I began to feel over-powered by them as I took a better look around me.

Blackberries were clearly winning the battle for survival in this area. They had huge bristly leaf clusters, thorns so sturdy they were almost triangular, and an abundance of green berries that would ripen too late for our use. Vehicles had been through often enough to keep a path clear between the encroaching briars here, but I looked along the line and could see them coming together farther down. I would not do much more walking here.

Down where the berry bushes seemed to be taking the clearing, I suddenly noticed cherry trees, some as tall as the light poles, an orchard of them along the forest edge. They were beginning to encroach on the blackberries. I had been puzzled last spring by the tiny white petals that dusted the service road so mysteriously. They were from the cherry trees that I had not even suspected were in the nearby power line clearing.

At hand, now that I was really looking and aware of cherry saplings, I saw trees at the edge of the forest with bright smooth bark and cherry leaves. They weren't yet as tall as I, and their trunks weren't much bigger around than the blackberry canes. But there were whole thickets of them. How had I ever over-looked the young cherry trees? And growing with them were maple and beech seedlings that were noticeable now as they became young trees.

Soon after that, the whine of power saws greeted us as we arrived. The power company was very much aware of the encroaching vegetation, and had to intervene to protects its installations. Crews cut smaller trees by hand, but they wid-ened the clearing, too, taking out more mature beeches and maples, narrowing the strip between the road and the clearing.

The next spring they sprayed the remaining shrubs and thickets of small trees with an herbicide. The power line strip took on the aspect of a disaster area. I averted my eyes from it as I walked the road. The following spring, buckwheat vines climbed the dead cherry trees and tripped me again as I walked the clearing. I found the pale corydalis blooming once more.

By summer the clearing was a wild flower garden. I found daisies, campions, St. Johnswort, spotted knapweed and other flowers of open places. But in a year the garden was gone. Berry bushes were rampant, taking over much faster this time since there was no traffic for firewood. The raspberry bushes weren't going to have a chance to produce pies, but there were a few berries to eat as I walked. Blackberry canes were already reaching out to bar my way, their sturdy barbs ready to jab through my clothing if I persisted. This corridor through the forest is a continuously shifting scene as one form of plant life crowds out another, nature against nature. There is also the contest of man versus nature. The mature forest was proceeding in its own ordained pattern until man intervened as he would have to do again and again.

Is this good? Or bad? The landscape has been altered for man. A twenty-five foot, mile-long strip of felled trees is certainly of no advantage to the forest. Nor does it add to man's aesthetic enjoyment of it. Its sole purpose is to allow man to bring the conveniences of civilization with him into the forest.

> Power.
> Power which makes it possible
> To banish the dark,
> Ignore sundown,
> Revel in unnatural night hours
> And sleep through the dawn.

Power to cook meat
Without holding it at the end of a stick
And building a fire under it,
To toast pale bread to
A nicety, automatically.

Power to keep warm by flicking a switch
With muscles too flabby
To cut wood
Or carry ashes.
Power to send water
Coursing through pipes
To the precise place of use,
And bathe feet too tender
To walk for it.

Power to sweep the floor,
Sew a seam, saw a board,
Open a can, brush teeth,
Shave beards, beat an egg.

Power to drown out
The sounds of wind,
Of rain, of singing birds,
With the voices of man
Saying, "Think thus,
Buy that, do this,"
To an acquiescent brain.
Power for all the things
Man would be healthier and wiser
To do for himself.

Power produced by using up
The natural world,
Power which further
Alienates him from nature,
Power which gives him more time to enjoy
What he has already destroyed
To gain.

Lord, even while condemning others, I am guilty, too. I am a purist about electricity in our cabin, while I use up other forms of energy. Tanks of bottled gas light our cabin and cook our food. Gasoline powers our boats. We burn gallons of precious fossil fuels traveling to and from our loved retreat.

In our zeal for an uncluttered simple life in the woods, we use paper towels and paper plates to save laundry and dish-washing. Trees must be cut to supply them. We are using up the forest even while we seek its shelter.

We buy prepared mixes, ready-cooked meals in boxes and cans, to give us more time on the lake, in the forest, heedless of the energy it takes to produce and package those products.

Let me not condemn others without examining my own life and actions. Forgive me. My only true source of power comes from you, the Almighty and Everlasting. I praise your name, now and forever.

Heart Of The Forest

I could no longer ignore the chipmunk chorus. Back in the hardwoods their cheerful chirking seemed to fill the woods, coming from every side. The morning sun was briefly touching stump tops and logs as it rose overhead and found chinks in the forest roof.

Extroverts of the woods, the little striped creatures proclaimed their presence loudly, moved noisily through the dead leaves of the forest floor. It takes no special skill to see chipmunks, even though their burrows are hidden. They are the friendliest and noisiest of wildlife. Ours are mostly the larger Eastern chipmunk with rusty rump and back, with five dark stripes. At the lakefront we see the smaller Western species, with a wiry tail as long as their bodies. Ours is one of the few areas where the ranges of the two chipmunks overlap. Chipmunks are all so easily tamed that it is a temptation to think of them as furry little parables, as Bergen Evans says in his "Natural History of Nonsense" we are apt to do.

We had heard that they sometimes fill their cheek pouches so full they can't get into their holes. To test this one day, we found an old-fashioned narrow-necked milk bottle, popped corn to put into it, and placed the bottle on its side in the firecircle. A chipmunk soon found his favorite food and didn't hesitate to enter the bottle.

"Now what's he going to do?" Fred asked the children who had come from next door to watch. The small animal's cheeks bulged fatter with the bulky kernels. The chipmunk tried to back out of the bottle again and again, but his cheeks were wider than the opening. Finally he dropped some of his load, squeezed out of the bottle and scampered off to his hole to store what was left.

Sometimes I wonder if we spoil our chipmunks. They don't have to work as hard to fill their winter storehouses, where they are said to store up to fifty times their own weight in food.

John Burroughs, watching from his study door at Woodchuck Lodge, put out two quarts of food one day and watched a chipmunk carry it, two pouchfuls at a time, to his den. At day's end it was gone, and he put the same amount out the next morning. It too disappeared. The chipmunk rested a day, but the next day, for the third time, he ran off with another two quarts. His stores must finally have been full, because he seldom left his den after that, and other chipmunks took his place at the feeding station.

Our chipmunks entertain us, and we could make parables of their industry, their greed. But they are animals in their own right and dignity, not playthings. I was startled to learn our friendly chipmunks are actually predators. They've been seen catching and eating snakes, salamanders, frogs, birds and mice. They are a threat to the grouse population because they roll the bird's eggs from their ground-level nests. The fox gets even with the chipmunks for depriving him of his favorite food, the grouse, by eating the chipmunks. No, chipmunks weren't created to entertain us, any more than the bear was created to furnish us with bearskin rugs.

I accepted the invitation of the chipmunk chorus now and entered the forest by the old logging track. On a broad maple stump ringed by new shoots, a chipmunk perched upright on its haunches and peered alertly back at me. This was his domain. In the firecircle the lively animals were in my territory, here I was invading theirs.

38

Signs that man had invaded the forest four years ago for timber cutting were everywhere. The tracks I followed were made by machinery used in that operation. The temporary roads had been very evident the first season. Now it was almost impossible to walk them, they were so choked with berry bushes and tree seedlings. It was even difficult to find the point of entry of most.

This track, because it went farther back into the woods, had been used by firewood gleaners. A few days ago I had decided not to try to push my way through the briars and young growth. Now it was again possible to walk it. Neighbors had made a path to the next lake so they could fish. I wouldn't follow it today, though, or I'd never get around the lake.

Last spring my friend Rita and I had hiked here when the woods were still quite open, the hardwoods just beginning to leaf out. A forest of young seedlings was springing up in the lumbering area, wherever sunlight reached a section of the forest floor formerly shaded by a mature tree. This brought new leaves and swelling leafbuds at convenient eye level for photographers and nature explorers.

I had long been aware of the rich flaming colors of new maple leaves. I had made many attempts to capture the scarlets and maroons on film, but spring colors were elusive. The most delicate shades of spring colors blended together on distant hillsides. The silvery, lacy aspen and the gauzy reds, yellows and greens of maple, birch and tamarack had spruce green exclamation points for contrast. On film it was all a washed-out pale green. Spring, yes. But not the spring I was trying to capture.

Bright colors caught my eye as I walked with Rita. "What's that?" I asked. "There's surely nothing blossoming here." Drooping plumes with satiny tints of red, bronze and gold adorned the ends of woody shoots. The sprouts were all coming from around a beech stump.

"Why, those aren't . . . they can't be . . . beech leaves couldn't possibly look like that. . . ," I stammered in my excitement.

"I don't know what else would be growing from a beech stump, do you?" Rita asked matter-of-factly. She already had her camera out.

"We shouldn't have any trouble getting those colors on film. They remind me of a bird of paradise blossom," I said.

We found new beech leaves photogenic in all their stages as we continued deeper into the woods. The fresh green deeply veined leaf surfaces and persistent golden bracts were symbolic of spring, especially when the sun shone through them.

"Oh, oh, oh!" I shrieked suddenly, on a rising crescendo.

"Now what?" asked Rita, waiting to see if she should get excited, too. "That was three 'Ohs.' Must be something special."

"I don't know what it is," I replied breathlessly, pointing to the ground.

"Well, at least you didn't jump up and down, too. You really set that sphagnum bog ajumping the other day. Let's have a look."

"There . . . by my toe, pushing up out of the ground like a bean, only it's a bright pink, like a Russula."

"Like a what?" Rita asked, following my pointing finger.

"A mushroom. That's the trouble when you start nature study with mushrooms. No one knows what you're talking about. What color would you call it?"

"Peony pink," Rita said, stooping for closer inspection.

I got down on my hands and knees to peer at the inch-high oddity. "Something's coming up, but what is it?" I asked.

There was no other pink object in sight. I did my best to get on a level with it, pushing my camera bag impatiently out of the way to lie prone on the ground. I saw a pink flush on the underside of leaves unfolding beside it, the cotyledons of some seedling. This was the next stage of development of whatever we were looking at. A tiny plume of future leaves was pushing up between the two original pink-flushed ones. But what were these leaves to be?

I sat up and looked around. "We're sitting under a beech tree, aren't we?" Rita asked.

"Yes, but I never saw a tree seedling like that," I said. I scratched in the loose duff of the path, a mixture of decomposing leaves and debris of all kinds. The largest particles I found were the burrs of beech nuts.

"I'll get a good record for identification," I said, and proceeded to photograph my find from every angle.

Later in the day I found more of the seedlings, with just enough pink to prove they were the same plant. Each time I found beechnut husks in the soil in which they grew, but when I examined the maturing second leaves they didn't have the parallel veins of the beech leaves we'd been photographing.

When the last color had faded from the sunset that evening and we could no longer see outdoors, we went in reluctantly to do the dishes. Then I tackled the nature guides I had brought along.

Tree books were no help. Leaves, bark, winter buds, flowers and fruit were all keyed to help in identification. None mentioned anything about the seedlings. Finally I dug an old Gray's Botany from the bottom of my book bag. It was a musty-smelling one I'd bought for ten cents at a book sale. There I found a drawing of our seedling. And it *was* a beech!

"Aha," I sighed in satisfaction. "I'd say we'd had a beechen day, wouldn't you?" I giggled at Rita's wary expression. "I searched the dictionary, too. That's the adjective form of 'beech.'"

The next morning I found a pinkish seedling under a beech tree near our own cabin.

41

I see. What a misused word, that small
word "see," making prevaricators of us all.

Of course I see that beech tree. I've seen
it from the window a million times, its smooth
gray trunk somewhat splotched with age.

I've walked under its branches, grateful for
green shade, shuffled through its cast-off
leaves of autumn bronze, oblivious of its brief
spring glory, the rainbow of color bursting
from long winter buds.

Glibly I've talked of beechnuts, having seen
nothing but empty, bristly shells, ignorant of
the triangular pair of meats it held, unaware of
the tree's beginning as an improbable pink
upthrusting from the forest floor.

Is it possible that if I look at anything long
enough, intently enough, I will see something
that I've not seen before?

"I see,"
I say sympathetically to a friend
who has told me his troubles.
Yet what do I really see
but a dim vision of a
mature, fruited situation?
What do I know of the roots,
the first glorious fruiting,
the blossoming,
the damaging storms,
the green growth of a problem.
I can only look and see

the obvious bulk of it and say,
"Yes, this is a problem,"
As I say, "Yes, this is a tree."
There is only one All-seeing Eye.

I came to a tangle of discarded logs and brush, with green vegetation engulfing it. The camouflage wasn't yet complete. The jagged ends of branches still reached out at grotesque angles. A chipmunk perched on a nearby snag gave a startled "chirk," then disappeared with a flick of its bottlebrush tail.

The litter from lumbering spoiled the beauty of the open-floored woods for me, but it gave excellent cover for wildlife. The closer to maturity a forest grows, the fewer animals and birds can live in it. What was to me mere inconvenience or unsightliness is to forest creatures shelter and food, the necessities of life.

I sniffed, smelling the sharp, acrid odor of fungi invading wood. I climbed into the tangle of logs, looking carefully before placing each foot. I spied small brackets and pulled aside vines. Covering the branch was a whole row of the woolly little brackets with the unpronounceable name *Schizophyllum*. They are worth any contortions necessary to see beneath them, because of the sculptured pattern of their double-edged rose-tinted gills. A row of miniature brackets sometimes adorns a stick. One winter I found persistent brackets in every winter thaw, becoming more beautiful each time the top of their log emerged from the snow. They assumed shapes and colors I had never seen in any book.

Fred laughed at my "affection for fungi." "I'm going to end my days living with a moldy old lady," he told friends. It is certainly true that I find myself smiling affectionately whenever I find these particular little brackets with the difficult name.

In the same brush pile now were some of the smooth papery

brackets with shining banks of silky orange hairs. New horses' hooves were sprouting on the remains of an old birch that had lost its lifehold in this mature forest before the loggers ever set foot here. This part of the hardwoods was taking the place of the power-line clearing now as my mushroom hunting grounds. It would become my laboratory during the years the fungi were at work reducing the brush piles to soil again.

The selective cutting operation had interrupted the natural processes of nature and changed the aspect of the forest. The wood that had been taken out in logs was for man's use, to be sawed into lumber or ground to pulp for paper. But in this case man by intervening had also benefited the forest. Without this intervention, it would gradually have passed from maturity to old age and fallen prey to decay, disease or storm. The new seedlings of maple and beech which clogged the woods were evidence that the forest was renewing itself.

Man had prolonged the life of the forest, renewed its vigor. It would again grow toward maturity instead of old age and death. In this case what is good for man is also good for nature. Man has studied nature's ways closely enough to work with it instead of against it, to use change as a tool.

Emerging from the hardwoods into the power line clearing again, I decided a few berry bushes shouldn't keep me from carrying out my original intention of walking the length of the clearing to Cassandra Marsh. I had traveled it easily two months ago in the spring.

I stooped under an arching cane which reached out to bar my way. Thorns caught the back of my jacket, one trouser leg was firmly snagged, and as I tried to free it my sleeve too was imprisoned. I wrenched violently free from them all with a feeling of panic. I licked the blood from the scratch on my hand and rolled down my sock to inspect the damage.

No wonder the dense black forests had terrified early settlers if a berry bush in bright sunlight could do this to me. Perhaps I should not so glibly condemn those who had looked upon nature as an enemy. I could have cheerfully hacked off that briar if I had had a hatchet.

That was enough of briars. I crossed the strip of remnant forest again to get back to the muddy service road.

The Conifer Swamp

I caught a glimpse of the lake as I looked through the forest to my left. I was walking along the part of the lakefront left unplotted for cabin sites. The reason was very evident now, because some of the trees were standing in water. Looking from the lake, as Fred and I do from a fishing boat, the area is dark green because of the conifers which predominate in the area. The swamp is usually dry enough to walk through, if I skirt the patches of wet moss and standing pools of water. I find mushrooms in the driest of seasons.

"Going to the swamp. Back in time to peel potatoes," I often scrawl on a scrap of paper for Fred. It is my favorite short jaunt from the cabin.

I chuckled to myself, slipped in the mud of the service road as I walked, and regained my balance. I was remembering the time I had taken a friend, newly arrived in the woods, along with me. After ducking past prickly hemlock branches, clambering over mossy logs, crawling under fallen trees and picking her way over old tree roots pockmarked with animal holes, my friend politely refused my next invitation to go hiking.

On the Forest Service map this is called a low wooded area. It is distinctly different from any other around the lake. In it I had found patches of the sphagnum mosses of the bogs, as well as a cluster of Labrador tea bushes among the Cassandra and sweet gale at the lake edge. Their leathery leaves, edges rolled down as if to protect the tawny fur undersides, were familiar to me because I had seen them in the swamp where Bob and Cora's log cabin trees had grown, surrounded by spongy sphagnum. Hemlocks and pines, alive and dead, with a sprinkling of hardwoods, justify my calling it a conifer swamp, even though it is a small one.

The area must shelter much wildlife. My only proofs are a red squirrel following me through the swamp scolding,—perhaps because he feared I'd filch the mushrooms he had stored in the crotch of saplings to dry—chipmunks going about their business, bear tracks but no bear, and a neighbor's pet raccoon coming and going from it. My expectation of high adventure has not been fulfilled.

The closest I came to an adventure was the day I walked through the swamp on an errand. Perhaps I was on my way to pick blueberries at the end of the lake, for I remember I didn't even have binoculars with me.

I ignored the loud bird noises overhead at first. Flocks of crows must be up there. The noise seemed to follow me and I decided crows weren't responsible. Listening carefully, I was hearing croaks, not caws. Those were ravens in the treetops, addressing their threats to a common target. Branches were so thick above me that I couldn't see the site of the commotion. I pushed through to the lakefront. Perhaps out in the open I could look back and see the treetops.

My first look upward as I reached the edge of the forest made me swallow my instinctive "Oh, oh, oh" in one long gasp. I set my uplifted foot down in slow motion. Above me, not ten feet away, a mature bald eagle perched on a branch. When Fred saw one wheeling in the sky, I had to take his word for it. But here, fierce yellow eye intent on the lake, its white head gleaming, here was my own eagle!

The ravens flapped over the forest on large black wings. The eagle took no more notice of my presence than he had of the ravens'. For what seemed a long time the eagle looked at the lake and I looked at the eagle.

I sat on a mossy hummock now, remembering. I've never seen an eagle here since. His habitat is threatened. His eyrie high in the tree in a remote forest area is being harassed by vacationers and cut down by lumbermen, and his food supply in the Great Lakes is becoming contaminated.

There is great concern over the future of the bald eagle in Hiawatha Forest. In 1974 only two nesting pairs were left, from seventeen such pairs in the early 1960's. Arch, our neighbor on the next lake, used to watch eagles rear their young every year in a huge nest high in a tall pine at the end of the lake. He watched the summer-long activity from his log cabin window. The pine was now fallen, the eagles gone.

It had been a long time since our blueberry picking in open places had been interrupted by Fred's cry, "There's an eagle," when he straightened up to stretch his tired back. It had been a welcome relief to look up and watch that distant bird circle up there in the blue over our heads.

Surveys show that eagles still nesting in the Upper Peninsula are doing so near uninhabited inland lakes, where pollution is slight and people are few. Recently a 3,500-acre forest and lake area northwest of us, site of one of the active nests, was posted closed to motorized traffic from March 1 to June 30. Though the pair nested and produced eggs, the eggs did not hatch, so the area was opened again in late May.

For the eagle its huge nest, added to yearly, is more than a place to lay and hatch eggs. I had seen killdeer eggs hatching in a nest as I hiked one day, and the next morning could not even find a sign of the nest's having been there. Not so with the eagle. The young do not leave the nest for ten or twelve weeks, are carefully tended by the parent birds, and even after they fly freely the plain brown young return and the nest is still headquarters for the whole family. After the first season the eaglets are on their own, taking four years to mature.

After a brief winter sojourn, usually in a warmer climate where water is open and fish can be caught, the adults return to their nest, long before egg-laying time. The structure has to be large to accommodate birds with wingspans up to seven feet. The nest itself is built of sticks and branches, but the two, sometimes three eggs are laid in a special nesting cavity lined with grass, mosses and feathers. Here the two adults share the incubation.

Remembering the austere, fiercely independent eagle that had perched here at the edge of our lake, I hoped he was one of the surviving ones still nesting somewhere in the forest. There is no danger of regarding him as a plaything, as we do the chipmunks. He is a memorable symbol, not only a national one but a personal one for me. How many times I have gained strength for an impossible task from Isaiah's words, "They that wait upon the Lord shall renew their strength; they shall mount up with wings as eagles."

> The eagle's eyrie is endangered,
> As is my woodland refuge.
> His need for solitude
> Is also mine.
> The food he eats to sustain life
> May kill him.
> Poison, disease-producing chemicals
> Are in my daily diet, too.
> He flies south in winter
> Looking for fishing sites,
> Roosts in sheltered valleys
> Near my winter home.
> We too are there for food and warmth

Where gardens grow and walls are snug.
But one thing I lack—
Those mighty wings.
I must wait upon you, Lord.
Only in your presence
Do I find new strength
With which to soar.

I left the eagle here, that long-ago day, still fishing. He was more expert that I at sitting and concentrating. Today I carried the memory with me as I walked back to the service road. The road wasn't much fun to walk this morning, but it was preferable to the water-filled swamp or the briar-choked power line clearing. I'd soon be at the place where the power line track branched off from the service road. The new opening made a large, sunny circle.

This clearing was alive with birds in the fall. Alone this would have been the extent of my memory. But Betty and Harry, who are devoting their retirement years to helping other people enjoy birds as much as they do, were with me one October.

From the golden tunnel of the service road we had stepped out into this clearing where we could see the sky . . . and the birds. Betty's binoculars were instantly focused.

"Purple finch," Betty said. "They don't settle long enough for me to get a good look, but I'd know that whispering song of theirs anywhere." Leaves were still on the trees, bright with color, and the rosy finches were blending into it.

Betty's skilled binoculars picked up myrtle warblers and a white-throated sparrow in the same place. My near-sighted, slow-focusing eyes did manage to see the yellow patches on one warbler, though the white throat of the sparrow escaped me.

I could enjoy the setting. The handsome old beech in fall bronze color was attracting the migrating flocks of birds with its ripe nuts. Maple leaves of red, yellow and green, the bright gold leaves of birch and the many-shaded textures of undergrowth, dominated by the deep wine of blackberry leaves, made the spot a rainbow of color. The birds were making it a rainbow of song.

Betty pulled her notebook from her pocket. "I must get these down before I forget. Let's see. In our three days here that makes forty species we've seen. At least those are the ones we've recorded."

"And in October!" I exclaimed. "I didn't think it was possible. I'll never forget the bluebird among fall leaves. Or that dear little winter wren." I had spotted the wren all by myself. Otherwise, I was happy with secondhand bird watching through Betty's binoculars.

"Don't forget the sharp-tailed grouse that posed in the road for us as we came in," Harry said.

"Once when we arrived after dark, as we turned in at the lake road we heard a whippoorwill calling so loudly that Fred stopped the car to listen. The bird was right in the middle of the road, in our headlights. We could see its movements, like a bellows, as it chanted," I said.

"We'll likely add some more birds to our list on our way out tomorrow," Harry said.

"You're sure you won't mind staying here alone when we leave?" Betty asked.

I reassured her. Few people understand how I treasure these brief solitary interludes in the woods. I looked forward to Fred joining me late Sunday night. But these times for assimilating my experiences and new knowledge, for thinking and just "being" are rare and precious. They are necessary to my enjoyment of people.

"I thank you so much for the bluebirds and warblers in October. I've never even looked for birds on our fall trips before."

"We've never been anywhere, at any time, that Betty didn't see birds," Harry said proudly.

"It's all in what you're looking for, isn't it? Do you remember that John Burroughs quotation about having the bird in your heart before you can see it in the bush? I've had friends tell me that after they've hiked the woods with me they begin to see mushrooms everywhere," I replied.

God above, you who created
This forest around me,
As well as the desert, the mountains,
The seas, the steppes,
The gorges and canyons,
The plains and the prairies,
The valleys and bogs,
The brook and the falls,
I find you here
Because you are already
In my thinking,
My breathing and doing.
I see you in a
Shaft of sunlight
Piercing morning mist,
The azure flash of a
Bluebird wing,
The fierce golden eye
Of an eagle,
The downy new
Leaf of the aspen,
The last flaming leaf
Of fall,
Because you are in me.

Spawning Marsh

If there were birds in the clearing they were silent now in the middle of summer, and the lush growth of green leaves would make birdwatching difficult for even Betty.

To the left of the service road the ground is higher again and reverts mostly to hardwoods. In the short distance before the slope down to the inlet stream, two lots had been laid out for summer cabins. Fred and I looked at them when we were deciding where to build. We would be alone down here at the end of the lake.

"Between two low areas the mosquitoes would be fierce," Fred said.

"But we'd see more deer," I said wistfully. "There'd be wildlife on all sides."

Though my early romanticism made it seem attractive from that standpoint, I knew now I had been relieved when Fred added, "The beach is weedy, and the curving shoreline must cut off the sunset views."

"It is sort of dark down here, isn't it?" I replied.

Only one of the lots had a cabin on it and for several years it had been secluded here at the dead end of the service road. But what a change now. The road that had been built across the marsh for the lumbering operation put the last cabin within a few minutes and a fraction of a mile from the highway joining Lake Michigan with Lake Superior. Instead of the most secluded, it had become the most exposed cabin.

Almost everyone used this new road now in preference to going the two miles around the lake. The Forest Service had offered to close it if that was the residents' wish. They had put a post in the middle of the road and installed a "Road Closed" sign. The post mysteriously disappeared, a practical way of voting. Now even those who favored isolation drove nonchalantly past the sign. I still felt a twinge of regret when Fred and I did, and I often urged Fred to use the longer road. Who needs to be in a hurry in the woods?

"But you aren't doing the driving over all the dips and ruts and high centers," my practical husband reminded me.

I had never completely oriented myself since the roadbuilding. Somewhere here had been an old beaver dam. Before we had come to the woods beavers had completely dammed the small stream that fed our lake. The evidence was there in the high mounds of a broken dam on either side. A ring of dead trees circling the marsh at the rim of the forest marked the high water of a former beaver pond. Rangers had undoubtedly discouraged the beavers, those industrious landscape artists who arrange things to their own liking.

I walked through the turnaround that used to mark the end of the service road, past the misleading "Road Closed" sign and out onto the raised roadbed. Fireweed, red-berried elder shrubs and alders were down at the marsh edge to the right. Piles of rotting logs sprouted brackets at the edge of the woods to my left. I stood on top of the large culvert, through which the stream now ran, and looked out into the marsh.

In spring when the spawning marsh had been in use, the area was flooded with shallow water. Now it was filled with a dense growth of shrubs, a pond of green leaves, with the narrow inlet stream making a channel through it. The stream was much as it had always been this time of year. I felt the hard roadbed under my feet and smiled. Not far from this spot, where the solid forest floor meets the less solid marsh, I had stood one summer taking pictures of wild flowers.

Camera to eyes, concentrating intently on the picture in the viewfinder, I had thoughtlessly moved one foot to get a different angle. I was thrown violently to the ground, one leg knee-deep in black muck. Fortunately the other foot was still on firm ground and I could pull myself free, still clutching my camera protectively. It must have taken a lot of rock and gravel to make a firm roadbed across that muck. Of course the culvert itself made a firm foundation at this point.

The Forest Service and the Michigan Department of Natural Resources had ingeniously made use of the culvert for wildlife management. They too in the spring dammed the stream and controlled its flow so that a pond formed. They were doing it in the best interests of the lake, men and fish.

Ranger Pete, the District Ranger, told me how they introduced either adult northern pike about to spawn, or northern pike fry into the marsh. A device in the end of the culvert made it possible to control the level of water and to prevent predator fish such as bass and perch from entering the marsh and eating the young pike as they hatched or were introduced.

When adult pike were introduced to spawn, they had to be removed after the eggs were laid to keep them from eating their own young. When fingerlings were of the proper size they were released into this lake by draining the pond or removed to stock other lakes in the area.

The stream was then allowed to flow naturally, as it was doing now. I was amazed at how little change there was in its short tree-lined distance from here to the lake. The tea-colored water still flowed in perceptible current in some places, was trapped in dark amber pools by fallen trees and branches in others, and eventually reached the lake. It was still the same stream I had crossed by means of fallen trees in our early years in the woods, while a red squirrel alternately scolded me and dropped pine cone scales on my head.

This certainly seemed to be a case of man making use of nature in a way beneficial to everyone, if you started with the fact that the culvert was already there.

> The beaver,
> Obeying the instinct
> Planted within,
> Goes about his business
> Of felling trees,
> Building dams,
> Forming pools
> Of the correct depth
> To favor him and his brood,
> Giving them the shelter and food
> Needed for survival.
>
> He creates new waterways
> For his exclusive use,
> Transports food and building materials
> To fill his own needs.
>
> Man, having been given
> Understanding, insight
> And compassion for his fellowmen
> As well as his fellow creatures,
> Has a responsibility
> To consider the needs of all.
> Yes, even I, Lord,
> Even I.

"Do you suppose it's still possible to walk through to the marsh stream from the turnaround?" I wondered. I'd have to try it someday. One evening in a dry season I had pushed through berry bushes and climbed over fallen tree barricades on the slope leading down into the marsh. The footing under the cattails, joe-pye weed, reeds and Cassandra bushes was comparatively solid. I had walked slowly out into the marsh through the shoulder-high vegetation, testing the ground as I went.

To my surprise, I soon found myself at the edge of the stream. It was a calm evening with no mosquitoes, and I decided this was a good time to see how long I could stand without moving. I knew there were marsh fowl in here. I had heard their strange croaking and cries in the spring over the chorus of spring peepers.

I watched the stream bank. Nothing moved. Very slowly I turned my head to inspect a nook to my left, sheltered by shrubs. It was several minutes before I realized there was a comical chicken-like bird right out in the open, rigidly looking at me. I stood with my mouth open, amazed, then laughed aloud, and the "chicken" was gone. It didn't take long to confirm in my bird books that I had seen a rail, though I wasn't sure what kind.

I was sure I had heard bitterns "pumping" in the marsh in spring. I was more anxious than ever to see one in "my own" marsh after I had gotten a good look at one on a bird club field trip at home. The ridiculous bird, two or three feet high, had frozen in an open field with his long bill held vertically, his stripes running up and down like reed stems, thinking he was safely hidden.

"There's probably a bittern out there right now, hiding in those reeds, looking me over as did the rail," I said to myself.

Last week Gladys and I decided to creep up on marsh birds in their own habitats by paddling up the stream in my new inflatable canoe. Our cameras were loaded with film and our telephoto lenses ready. We carried the canoe down the service road and floated it in the small pond at the culvert. It was like riding in a life preserver once we were in, but the boat had a strong tendency to carry my feet out from under me when I tried to board it. I sat in the edge of the pond suddenly with an extremely loud splash.

I was aware of two things, Gladys' startled face as she rushed to help me, and the camera bag on my hip. I pushed aside Gladys' offer of assistance. "My camera," I gasped, struggling to get the strap over my head. "Quick. Take it." Gladys understood. She grabbed Kleenex from her pocket, opened the bag and applied first aid.

"Is everything ruined?" I asked desperately as I sat there in the pond. I had several hundred dollars worth of equipment in that bag, all vulnerable to water damage.

"Nope," Gladys said brightly, dumping water out of the bag. "Just a few drops on the outside of things. I've dried them off. And now how about getting out of that pond? Here I was worried about you, and all you could think of was your camera. By the way, are you okay?"

I gave a relieved laugh and stood up dripping. "Just shook up a bit. These jeans will drip-dry if the label is correct," I said, "but do you still want to sit in that small boat with me?"

We stopped when we were only a few yards into the winding stream. There was no firm footing on either side, and most certainly none in the muck of the stream bottom. A log barred our way and unyielding Cassandra twigs scratched both sides of our fragile boat. We could not remove the log or lift the boat over, and there were bound to be similar barriers ahead. We had to back out.

Since our proposed journey had proved impossible, we floated for a while near the culvert. We saw plants growing on the banks and around the edge of the small pool that we hadn't noticed before, now that we were at eye level with them, seated comfortably on a cushion of air.

"Look. Those leaves have the five fingers of cinquefoil," I said to Gladys, maneuvering our airy boat in the inlet stream so

58

I could reach out for a specimen. "I thought they all had yellow blossoms, but these are purple."

"Marsh cinquefoil," my flower book said. The large purple parts aren't petals, but the sepals that contain them. The petals, inside, are smaller. "Pretty, aren't they?" I said to Gladys. "And they're growing right where they belong, according to the book, in wet meadows."

"There's another blossom I've not seen before," I said, pointing to a small white bloom on an erect stem. "And it's right here at the culvert where I've stood so many times birdwatching."

"It has three symmetrical petals," Gladys said, "around a prominent green center. Here's the leaf." She reached out and isolated one leaf in the palm of her hand. "Looks like arrowhead, doesn't it?"

My book on pond vegetation confirmed our identification later. The common name is duck potato because the roots are a staple food of waterfowl. Muskrats like them, too, and Indians used to raid muskrat houses in the marshes for their store of tubers.

The muskrats I watched from the culvert one August morning undoubtedly knew about them. They seemed more interested, though, in the large cattail marshes that covered the banks of the stream where it came out of the forest on the far side of the marsh.

I had come to the culvert early one morning for bird watching and found the birds silent. The sun was not yet reaching the marsh. But I saw ripples moving toward me from the stream, then a small dark head at the center. I stood motionless as a muskrat reached the culvert beneath my feet and disappeared. I moved quickly to the other side in time to see the animal emerge, swim unconcerned on down to the tangle of logs in the stream, scramble out upon the bank and disappear into the dense undergrowth. It reappeared a few yards to my right, where the forest met the road.

The name muskrat is an unlovely one. The Indian word "musquash" that Thoreau often used in his journals is better. The state of Louisiana in 1944 passed a law renaming the animal the "marsh hare." I studied the "rat" as it posed unconcerned at the roadside, and agreed with those who were more familiar with it than I. It was more like a plump, overgrown meadow mouse than a rat, the body about a foot long, if you didn't count the mouse-like tail. The muskrat's fur is used to make handsome coats. This animal's coat was still dark and wet from the stream as it huddled on its haunches to eat some unidentifiable food. Perhaps it had found a mussel on the banks of the stream to supplement its vegetable diet.

Animal books carry a warning that muskrats are apt to be belligerent on land and sometimes attack people they think threaten them. This fellow gave no sign that he even knew I existed. Once a visiting friend who had gone for an early morning hike while I planned the day's activities reported seeing two muskrats, evidently an adult and immature one, by the outlet stream. The small muskrat had approached curiously and sniffed at her shoelaces as she stood motionless.

My muskrat disappeared into the forest and I turned to the stream again. Another set of ripples approached. I could see the triangular head, the rounded hump of the body and a naked narrow tail undulating behind. Since the tail is flattened vertically it makes an efficient rudder, and the webs on the bottom of the hind feet send the muskrat smoothly through the water. Front feet are tucked under its chin, until the claws are used to scuttle up banks.

I must have made some movement that betrayed my presence. The animal dove, the ripples disappeared. Muskrats can stay under water twelve minutes, which is longer than any of their predators, and gives them a defense against them. I waited. Finally the "musquash" emerged at the mouth of the culvert, scrambled quickly over the rocks and into the water, came out the other side of the culvert and dove out of sight near the bank.

I turned to inspect the marsh again, hopeful that birds might begin to respond to the growing daylight. A third muskrat came downstream from the unseen cattail beds. Perhaps it was the light that made this one more cautious. It disappeared underwater, and then scrambled to hide in the marsh vegetation. The birds seemed in no hurry to sing. Before I left for the cabin and breakfast, the third muskrat finally made its way through the culvert to disappear after the others.

The stream flows through a strip of dark forest before emerging into the lake, and its banks are doubtless a honeycomb of tunnels with many entrances protected by the roots of forest trees, many underwater. I have not seen a typical domed muskrat lodge in our marshes. Muskrats swimming in the lake at dusk are a common sight. The last glow of sunset accentuates the ripples they make, expanding to fill the lake before they disappear.

Patches of sheered bulrushes at the lake edge show where muskrats feed, and on a late evening boat ride I once heard them crunching the rushes. Perhaps they have the best of both worlds, with headquarters in the stream that gives them access to both the marsh and the lake, to both cattails and bulrushes.

If our muskrats have stores of duck potato tubers, I thought now as I stood remembering, they must be in the tunnels of the stream banks. As I looked again at the arrowheads at the pond's edge, I saw bur reeds growing with them, their round green seedheads covered with green spines. Interesting texture, I noticed, taking a look at the direction of the sun. Especially with a low sidelight. I would come back another time, late in the day, for a photograph. A turtle slid off a log into the water as I adjusted the camera strap to a more comfortable spot on my shoulder and picked up my hiking bag.

Honeysuckle Landing

The new roadbed soon joined the original road to this end of the lake, but in its short distance it had completely altered the landscape. There used to be a long, gradual slope down to the stream here, wooded, carpeted with pine needles, old leaves and moss. Somewhere near, either under the road or in the bare spot where sand had been gouged out for use in roadmaking, Fred and I had found "beefsteak" mushrooms.

Arch, our neighbor and a native of the area, had confirmed our find. "Man, are they good, soaked overnight in salt water and cooked like morels. Everybody in the 'U.P.' looks for them in the spring. Come about the time of morels, a bit earlier maybe."

The red-brown crinkly masses were our first venture in wild mushroom eating beyond the morels Fred had hunted in Illinois woods. They were also my first mushroom photography.

Later, when study took me beyond merely comparing pictures in books, I discovered that *Gyromitra esculenta*, in spite of the name and the fact that many people eat the fungus, contains a harmful chemical. Pre-soaking and thorough cooking makes it possible to eat beefsteak mushrooms without visible harmful effects. But because of the long range effect on blood corpuscles they are a questionable food. Later, I learned that mycologists have found even more harmful substances in the Gyromitras.

I was uneasy about people eating beefsteak mushrooms,

and relieved when I found someone was doing something about it. That someone was my friend Ingrid whom I met on a mushroom foray. Ingrid's job was consumer marketing, and her area the Upper Peninsula. A survey Ingrid conducted on wild mushroom eating habits thoroughly alarmed her. A bloodcurdling array of folk tales and "sure" tests came to light. Nothing but luck saves most mushroom hunters from a horrible death because of eating poisonous species.

Ingrid began a campaign. "Eat only when you know the species with scientific certainty," she said. Even then, constant vigilance in picking and sorting is a necessity. A deadly Amanita, carelessly broken off above its telltale cup, can easily be mistaken for an edible pasture mushroom.

"I read in the paper the other day that eating beefsteak mushrooms is dangerous," Arch said one spring. "I've quit." I was relieved. Ingrid was being heard. I didn't tell Arch that Fred and I had quit several years ago. I was only a "tenderfoot," not an expert. I still find the mushrooms on the slopes farther along the edge of the marsh and admire their beauty. They look so unbelievable when I come upon them sitting there on the ground.

Arch and his wife had found the care of their lake acreage too much for them in recent years and moved to the Soo to make their home. We missed them. When I became too absorbed in trying to identify a mushroom or wandered off for bird-watching, Fred would say, "Guess I'll go see Arch." Now the friendly gate was locked and the cabin boarded up, another symbol of the change in our northwoods life.

In looking for beefsteak mushrooms I made other discoveries. When the spawning marsh was new I had pushed along its farther slopes in the spring. The pond spread out to cover the whole marshy area then, and water reached to the bottom of the slope. Shallow water covered the roots of the shrub border.

Birds flitted in and out just above the water, too elusive for my inexperienced bird-watching. With perseverance I finally saw the spotted breast of one often enough to be sure it was one of the thrushes which must have a nest nearby or be building one.

Satisfied, I walked on till I came to the power line stretched across the marsh. There in the shallow water were the stumps of trees cut to make way for it. Each one was topped with a bright little island of British soldier lichens, with enough silvery gray reindeer lichen mixed with it for contrasting color and texture.

Usually the soldier lichen clusters are so small that people walk on them without seeing them. They are rarely over an inch high and usually less. Their red caps probably give them their name, though they are only the size of the head of a pin. With a hand lens you can see the caps have a variety of shapes that certainly would not pass military inspection. In dry weather they are found in isolated little clusters, stems more gray than green, their bright caps subdued.

Finding large areas of them in a rainy season is a treat. I once found a log with a garden of British soldiers marching down the ridges of the bark—several detachments of them, in fact. The stump tops, looking like floating islands at the edge of the marsh pond, were the most picturesque I have ever seen.

The mosquitoes were fierce that spring. I put a net over my head, with insects clinging to my hands and wrists as I tied the string. Then I renewed the mosquito dope on my hands from a spray can in my pocket. This was no time to stop for photographs, and trees were shading the area at this time of day anyway. Actually it was fall before I got back to take the picture and I was able to walk out into the drained marsh then.

Now, in the mosquito-free summer, I stood in front of the maple tree where I had seen an unfamiliar bird perch in the spring. The tree was out in the open at the end of the lake.

udier hues in my imagination

it with a shining iridescent

re. Since Rita had seen it

ed at an identification, I was

nory of a delectable, many-hued

books.

ckdrop of green and blue

plashes her paintpot with discretion.

et is not wasted on the bulk of a bear,

ut saved for the tanager

That flashes briefly between white birch boles.

A vermilion mass of mosses would be gaudy,

While pinpoints on lowly lichens please the eye.

The red berries of wintergreen,

Mountain ash and elder

Announce "Here is food" to forest creatures,

And soon are gone.

Maroon of maple buds,

Cerise of beech, winter red of osier

Are soon engulfed in spring's green tide.

True, all are massed in the extravaganza of fall,

When scarlet and maroon

Are measured by the mile

And all rules are laid aside,

But wise nature doesn't let it last.

Fall wind, a giant eraser, blows away, in a day,

Scenes almost pleasanter to remember than to see.

In memory you need not shade the eye.

The sun was well out over the lake now, beaming directly down on me between the scattered trees. I didn't need my jacket, but since shedding it involved removing binocular and camera straps from around my neck and the heavy camera bag from over my shoulder, I would wait until I stopped to rest.

This was the highest part of the lakeshore and
the highway. An access road a fourth of a mile long
handiest place for fishermen to launch boats. In
there were usually boats from area resorts pulled
beach for the use of patrons, or for rent to fishermen.
I had rented one our first year in the woods. Now tha
boats are towed by vacationers, it is the boat launching ar
parties coming in to fish the lake for a few hours or a day

Over the weekend, three camping trailers had been park
here, plus a tent or two, evidently a party of family or friends
They had a lovely view of the whole length of the lake, and the
boat landing was handy.

"They could not only see the whole lake; here on this exposed spot, the whole lake could see them," I thought as I stood
where the camp had been. I felt embarrassed when Fred and I
drove through on Sunday morning, taking the shorter exit road
so we wouldn't be late for church twenty-five miles away.

"But if everyone wanted seclusion there wouldn't be any
secluded places left, would there?" I said to Fred as we followed the road through the grassy pine plantation to the highway.

"The campgrounds we pass always seem so crowded," I had
said to friends at home, who pulled a camping trailer to Michigan each summer at vacation time.

"We're farmers and work by ourselves most of the year. On
vacations we enjoy the out-of-doors, but we also want to be
with people. We like close neighbors when we camp. The
fellowship and new friends are part of it."

"I'd not thought of that," I said, feeling my mind stretch as I
looked through another's eyes.

"We can understand, though, how you and Fred, who spend
your lives working with people, enjoy solitude on your vacations."

"I hope you had a wonderful time on our lake," I said now to

66

the weekend campers who had been here. "A rather belated thought," I mused, "but at least it makes me feel better."

Sometimes it was difficult to have kind thoughts for a few of the campers. Of late years wheel tracks made a road off to the right of the boat landing, where people come in with trailers and tents, or sometimes just drive in for a Saturday night campfire.

The last are apt to be the disturbing ones. A huge campfire lights the lake about the time it is full dark, and sounds of revelry last well into the night. The next time I hike that way, I find beer bottles tossed into the sweet fern and blueberry bushes, or lately piles of cans, sometimes partially buried and sometimes not, and occasionally a bit of discarded clothing.

It is unlikely that the Forest Service policy of providing diverse recreational opportunities stretches to include providing a setting for this type of recreation. When people camp in a tent or park a trailer to stay some time on the lake, they are usually here to enjoy the woods and lake, as are we and our neighbors.

I walked down to the boat landing to see if the northern bush honeysuckle was still blooming. Last week Gladys and I had been exploring when I'd spied a yellow blossom on a low shrub near the path. The pointed leaf seemed familiar to me, and I realized that I had seen these bushes many times without even wondering what they were. Gladys and I were here a week earlier than I had hiked the woods before, and I was seeing them in bloom for the first time.

The small yellow or orange trumpets of the honeysuckle are not showy, and there are not many to a bush. Since then I have seen bush honeysuckle in many places. They are especially plentiful in low masses along the two miles of the original entrance road which I had hiked many times on the way to and from the mailbox, and which we'd driven too many times to count.

Honeysuckle. Why, I'd seen a showy bloom, a dark red one, on some scattered vining bushes in an open place just past the outlet stream in the spring. I even photographed the bright clusters of waxy berries in their setting of paired leaves in August. Come to think of it, just last spring I had found small white blossoms almost buried in the thicket of new maple seedlings beside our own lane, and discovered a Tartarian honeysuckle bush growing there.

I had always thought of honeysuckle as belonging in old-fashioned gardens. I would have to revise my thinking if there were three species here around this northwoods lake and even more in the Michigan shrub book.

"There is so much yet to learn" I said in despair to Gladys. My ignorance seems to grow apace with my knowledge, I thought.

> Oh, Lord, that I may truly know,
> Make me aware of my ignorance.
> That I may truly see,
> Awaken me to my blindness.
> That I may truly hear,
> Show me how rarely I listen.
> That I may truly feel,
> Pierce through my insulation.
> That I may fully taste of life,
> Set me athirst with humility.

Lookout Trail

The sandy camper tracks took me still higher above the lake as I followed them. Shaggy grass carpeted the open woods, with large patches of low blueberry bushes, dark green sweet fern shrubs, and occasional oak seedlings or old stumps.

To my left the ground sloped steeply down to the lake where bushes grew more thickly and trees formed a border. I remembered looking out over the blue blue lake one spring through a fringe of red-budded maples, lacy new aspen leaves and long needles of pine. A dainty forest of quaking aspen had been at my back, giving off glints of sunlight as their shiny new leaves whirled in constant twinkling motion.

Sturdy oak trees grew here, the only area bordering our lake where I found many of them. They are more at home in meadows and grasslands than in the deep woods around the cabins. In late fall when trees are bare and the large masses of color only a memory, bright leaves of the oak seedlings in the faded grass and the deep burgundy of huckleberry bushes hugging the slopes in chill winds are a lingering remembrance of autumn.

Reindeer lichen and wintergreen covered the ground as I left the path to examine a Juneberry bush, a magnificent one twice my height, which had been in full bloom last spring. Standing by itself here in the open it had a beautiful symmetrical shape and was easy to spot. I am always amazed in the spring to see how many of the bushes there are along the lakefront of the cabin area. Crowded in among other trees and shrubs, they go unnoticed until they blossom.

Juneberries bloom only a short time and it is a treat to be in the wood when they do. Only a few times have I found them at their peak. One year I went trigger happy, taking picture after picture of the white blossoms against the blue spring lake. In the woods the shadbushes, as they are also called, do not seem to bear fruit. I pulled branches of this bush down to eye level and found a few stray dark red berries still hanging. Fred and I are rarely in the woods at fruiting time, but the one pie we made from sugar plums, as Arch calls them, had oozed with rich sweet juice.

This reminded me that I was hungry. Just ahead was the spot I liked to use for a leisurely inspection of the lake. It is the highest of the open grassy campsites. I remembered huddling here on the slope to the lake in October, well below the brow of the hill, to be out of the cold wind, munching an apple, feeling the welcome warmth of the sun.

Today I took off my hat, removed my jacket and used it for a cushion as I chose a patch of shade near the top of the slope. The cooling breeze was welcome now. I was wearing a cast-off shirt of my son's which had worn so thin the breeze moved through it freely. I have found that the usual vacation attire of shorts, sleeveless blouses and sneakers are not for me. I would soon be a mass of scratches, barked shins and, in spring, insect bites. With stout shoes and socks, jeans and protected arms I can take off for the densest woods or briar patch at a moment's notice.

I felt a bump as I shifted to a more comfortable position away from the twigs of the blueberry bushes, and realized it was the apple in my jacket pocket. Fall or summer, this was a good spot for the juicy fruit. And for quiet contemplation. I find it difficult to take time for this on a hike. Always there is the feeling of

70

urgency, so much yet to see, to discover. This is when I quote my friend Anna to myself.

"Take it easy. Relax. There's so much to discover right where you are. Look closely." While others rush excitedly from one marvel to another, Anna becomes intimately acquainted with one blossom, one leaf.

I remember with delight, whenever I need it, the cold November day that Anna and I, warmly clothed, sprawled around a rotting stump in a Forest Preserve at home. We spent the better part of an hour on the cold ground, warmed by our enthusiasm, as we explored every cranny and crevice and root of the decomposing wood for fungi, insects, lichens and mosses. Hand lenses had magnified the many wonders.

We belong to different generations, and the years have taken their toll of Anna's hearing, but she more than makes up for it with seeing and deliberately savoring the things most people overlook. I realize it is good for me to have to curb my eager hiking stride to match Anna's slower one. Once Anna had walked this lake with me.

"Remember," Anna had said, laughing and out of breath, "that your legs are longer than mine. What you step over I have to crawl under."

I would look with Anna's eyes while I rested. I didn't have to look far. There by my blue-denimed knee was a bed of moss, its usual star pattern interrupted by its fruiting. I used my hand lens, so small it would fit inside a walnut shell, to explore the miniature world of mosses. The red ribbon by which the lens can hang around my neck, twist around a jacket button or loop through a buttonhole dangled brightly as I leaned over the moss. The conspicuous color keeps me from absent-mindedly laying the lens down and walking off without it.

One June, looking through Anna's eyes introduced me to an insignificant little "weed" whose blossoms are so small you step on them without realizing you are walking in a flower bed.

Under the magnifying lens they were miniature bouquets of stars. Bemused at the time by mushrooms, I casually identified the small plants as Houstonia, relatives of the bluets. Then I was rudely awakened to my unscientific botanizing. Houstonias have four petals, so how could they be stars? Finally I identified the mystery flower as bastard toadflax, and almost wished I hadn't. What a horrid name to wish on any plant!

In August I had been challenged by another insignificant low-growing plant with blossoms that were almost hidden. Having once noticed them, I found they were the most prevalent flower wherever I walked. Specimens wilted before I got back to the cabin. Down at the lakefront one evening I found the blossoms at my feet as I tried to identify an elusive bird flitting in and out of the sweet gale bushes. I raced to the cabin with the fragile flower and traced its whitish-yellow tubelike structure to the snapdragon family. Its common name is cowwheat. I dedicated the miniature to Anna.

I retrieved the apple I had laid aside to use the hand lens. M-m-m-m. It was crisp and juicy, as an apple should be, and waxy smooth in my hand. The stump felt good against my back, too. I develop odd cricks in my neck and back after a session with the hand lens or close-up camera lenses.

There is also a time for stretching the eyes to the horizon. I didn't want to get lost in the microscopic world. The panorama of the lake was before me. From looking long and looking small I must in turn look long, look large, look far.

A blue and green world it was that I looked at, the world Fred and I live in for at least a month each year. The green of the forest stretched to the horizon and bordered the whole lake, and the green of nearby oak and pine branches framed the picture. The blue of the sky and lake was by far the larger expanse, with green separating the two shades.

From the firetower, now replaced by patrol planes, the reverse was true. You looked out into a sea of green interrupted

72

here and there by small puddles of blue, which were our and neighboring lakes. My world, hiking in the forest, is green with the blue background of sky seen through trees. Fred's, fishing the lakes, is blue with green.

The colors of earth, someone has called them. Life itself began in the blue of the seas, cannot exist without water. The very breath we breathe comes to us from the oxygen-producing green of leaves and grass. A lovely thought. I thanked the unknown donors of it.

The bank on which I was sitting was about twelve feet above the level of most of the lakefront. This was the wide part of the lake, and the deepest. The snag where the eagle perch used to be was above my head somewhere. Early morning fishermen used to report seeing an eagle, and one day I had seen it with my own eyes from our own dock. I had been sweeping the shoreline with my binoculars when the sun came over the treetops behind me and highlighted the white head of the large bird. What a much better view he had than I. But the eagle wasn't interested in views. He concentrated intently on fishing.

This reminded me. "I wonder how Fred is doing over on Blue Joe?" I thought. "Hope he's catching fish and not stuck in a mudhole on the way in." Catching fish is his absorbing interest, too. Parishioners who kid him about his hobby are reminded, "I'm not doing anything Peter didn't do." If they look puzzled, he quotes John 21:3, "Simon Peter said to them, 'I am going fishing.'"

Once when Fred returned from his Canadian trip, a parishioner who lived next door to the parsonage installed a sign on the parsonage lawn, "Fish for sale." Sunday morning's announcements included one that the preacher had intended sharing his catch with his neighbor, but he was now making it known he'd sell the fish for what it cost him, five dollars a pound! Taking into account the cost of a three-thousand-mile

73

round trip, food and lodging and boat for a week plus Canadian license, this was probably the most expensive food we ate.

Fred didn't fish this lake much anymore, and neither did the eagles. They both share an interest in northern pike. The eagle does not eat fish exclusively. When he soared over our blueberry patch, he may have been looking for small mammals or land birds. When eagles fly south for the coldest winter months, December through February, the largest concentrations are on the large river systems where they can find fishing in open water. But eagles also winter in the large land areas of the southwest, including the desert, where their diet varies.

Not even the experts are sure where the bald eagles from our Upper Peninsula area winter. Most migrating birds have been traced through banding. The bald eagle, largest North American bird of prey except for the California condor, with its deadly beak and talons designed for clutching and shredding flesh, defies trapping. Young eaglets are banded in nests, but few are recovered so their movements can be studied. Eagle researchers working in Saskatchewan have finally gathered enough information about wintering locations to learn that birds nesting there fan out in a triangular pattern down in the States, from Montana and California on the west to Missouri and South Dakota on the east.

If eagles from Upper Michigan do the same, I could imagine some of them, possibly even the one from our lake, ending up in the Mississippi Valley on the western leg of their triangle. I have seen a deep ravine along the Mississippi River which gives shelter from prevailing winter winds where as many as fifty eagles congregate to roost in the three winter months.

Winter shelter is as important as nesting sites. Exposure to severe weather causes the eagle to use up stores of fatty tissue for energy. In these tissues are concentrated the poisons from industrial wastes and pesticides. The poison comes from the fish he eats which in turn have fed upon contaminated animal and vegetable life in the polluted water of our lakes and streams. If these poisons are absorbed into his body too fast, they even more severely limit his reproductive capacity.

All of our eagles, however, do not go south. Friends of ours have a delightful home on a forest lake. The picture windows in every room of their house look out upon the lake and National Forest that surround them. Baldy Lake, where eagle nesting sites have been protected, is not far away. One winter they reported they had often seen as many as three eagles fishing where a small open stream enters the lake near their home. The warmer water of the stream melts the ice around its mouth, and here the eagles find food.

Do they find enough food so that the poisons already accumulated are not released into their bodies? Are the eagles better off in a sheltered climate where fish are contaminated, or in the severe northland winter with food from clear inland lakes? The Forest Service seeks an answer to this, hoping that the extra food they provide the eagles in the way of highway killed deer in the winter will bring proper balance to the eagles' predicament.

There really is no safety for eagles anywhere, even though their only enemy is man. Since bald eagles are on the endangered species list, there is a stiff fine for shooting one. But there are other ways in which we endanger them without realizing it.

As I sat pondering the eagle's plight, I was looking toward the other end of our lake, three-fourths of a mile away. It narrows somewhat like an extension of the small end of an egg and is quite shallow, although the shoreline in no way resembles the smooth outline of an egg. Even though the lake is small, there are coves and inlets hidden from view from any vantage point. The lakefront to my left as I rested is the most irregular and heavily forested. I am glad it was chosen for the cabin sites. The many indentations give a feeling of privacy; except for our west cove neighbors we are not aware of other cabins at all.

Another reason for the choice had undoubtedly been that

trees hide the buildings from the lake. The terms of our lease of forest land require that any building be one hundred feet back from the shoreline, and that the lakefront must be left in its natural state.

I rejoiced that this careful planning had succeded so well. If it weren't for the boats pulled up to the beach or overturned on the shore, a stranger might fish the lake without realizing summer homes are there. When dusk comes, lights glint in a friendly way through the trees, marking human habitations for those who are still on the lake fishing or paddling a canoe in the moonlight. Campers on the lake are much more obvious, as the sites are open.

When we first built our cabin I discovered an edition of Thoreau's *Walden* in the library, illustrated with photographs by Edwin Way Teale. Several of the pictures were so like our own lake that I asked a bookfinder to locate an out-of-print copy for me. Our lake is even the same size as Walden Pond. Since the shores of Walden seem to rise higher above the lake than most of ours, it is from where I was sitting that our lake most resembles the photographs.

I realized that much of our lakefront is only a few feet high. In several places it is barely inches above the water, accounting for the intermittent marshy and swampy areas which give so much variety to my circuit of the lake.

I heard the muffled sound of a motor, the slam of a car door. Clanking sounds told me that someone was launching a boat on our lake, down at the boatlanding where I had just been inspecting the honeysuckle.

I heard the clatter of an outboard motor and the boat nosed out into the lake. The wake of the fisherman's boat spread wider and wider as he anchored in the pike hole. Some of the ripples merged into the half of the lake riffled by a light breeze, the others disturbed the reflections in the calm area not reached by the wind. The quiet part of the lake was a softer blue and reflected an occasional floating white cloud. I watched these clouds, mesmerized by their slow drifting, forming and re-forming.

The apple core would make food for chipmunks or squirrels. I tossed it off into the blueberry bushes, leaned back against the stump and gave myself to the moment. The breeze blew soothingly through my shirt, lifted the hair gently back from my face.

> Blow, wind of God.
>> Blow away the buzzing doubt,
>>> the stinging slight,
>>>> the feverish thought,
>>>>> the burning word.
>>>>>> Blow away all thought of self,
>>>>>>> Of daily care.

> Where is the wind?
>> Where leaves are stirred,
>>> Waves whipped to froth,
>>>> Brows cooled,
>>>>> Sails caught,
>>>>>> Sand shaped into dunes.

> Where is God?
>> Where lives are changed,
>>> Men stirred to action,
>>>> The impossible accomplished
>>>>> Rest comes to the weary,
>>>>>> Respite to those in pain—
>>>>>>> These are the visible evidence
>>>>>>>> Of an invisible God.

> As the wind is seen moving the treetops,
> O God, may you be seen at work in me.

Cassandra Marsh

I stretched. Time to move. Nothing dramatic had happened here. No lumbering, power line or spawning marsh altered the landscape. The sandy trail by which cars could now reach the campsite seemed the only change. A small trailer or tent sometimes stood in the open place overlooking the lake, a temporary part of the scene. When it left, the grass, the blueberry bushes, the mosses, the white pine and birch at the lakefront and the oaks on the ridge were as before.

"Or are they?" I suddenly wondered. I walked diagonally down the slope to intersect the path campers had made, leaving my gear scattered where I had rested. My feet sank over my shoetops into deep, loose sand as I followed the path, slipping and sliding, to the lake.

I looked back to the top of the slope. The first feet had walked through grass and mosses to launch a boat or to get water to drown a campfire. Many feet followed and wore off the grass. As use increased, new growth was discouraged. Friction eventually wore away all the ground cover, then the layer of roots and the inch or so of humus which plants need to grow.

There was only sand left and nothing to hold it. Feet pushed it downhill as they walked, rain washed it out, hollowed the path deeper and deeper. Soon the easiest way to get to the lake would be to sit down at the top and slide. The sand deposited at the bottom made a tiny beach, handy for boat launching. But it definitely altered the landscape. As I looked along the lakefront to my right I could see another raw sandy gash in the wooded shoreline, leading to another campsite.

Wherever men go they make trails. I remember seeing an old map of the lake as it was thirty-five years ago, with only the short road into this west end of the lake and another to the campsite at the opposite end which likely served also as a fire road. A certain number of trails are needed to give access to remote areas in case fire is spotted by rangers in lookout towers or patrol planes.

At the time we discovered our lake there were roads giving access to each side of it—though "trail" would be a better description since none of the roads was more than two sandy wheel tracks with a grassy center. A road had been added to give public access to the swimming beach directly across the lake from our cabin where now camping sites could also be used. The trail giving access to the east end of the lake had been extended all along the north shore, back of the lots laid out for cabins, ending in the turnaround. They had to be cut through the forest.

We used to feel we were safe and secluded in our cabin area, even though we were close enough to hear cars on the graveled highway when the wind came from that direction. The marsh lay between, a symbol of all that separated me from that other world. The year the graveled highway was blacktopped we were distressed by the sounds of bulldozers and heavy machinery invading our wilderness, even from a distance, and relieved when quitting time came and night brought only the natural sounds of the forest.

The marsh was no longer the barrier it once had been. The road made to carry lumber out now made it possible for campers formerly isolated from us to take evening strolls down the marsh road and the service road back of us. Sightseers could drive through freely.

When neighbors got together, the subject of the deplorable state of the entrance road was sure to come up. The Forest Service promised us a road, but was under no obligation to improve it. I was perfectly happy with it the way it was.

There were times when Fred didn't completely agree with me. When we arrived with a loaded car we hit bottom as the sandy ruts wore deeper. After a heavy rain we had to drive out into the blueberry bushes and sweet fern and hidden stumps to keep the brakes dry, because the road disappeared occasionally into small ponds. Always we had to bounce slowly over the exposed rocks on the ridges.

Before I start deploring trails made for the use of others, I thought, I had better realize that our family cabin, with all it has meant to us through the years, would not be possible without roads by which to reach it.

> Man was created to walk the earth,
> And where his feet trod, a path was made,
> Even in the Garden of Eden.
> A round stone of its own momentum
> Rolled down a hill,
> And man, observing, made a wheel
> Which carried him and his loads
> Farther and faster than his feet.
> He saw four-footed creatures
> Skimming the earth more swiftly than he,
> And bade them pull the wheels,
> Making wider trails, packing hard the earth,
>
> Man used his fertile brain
> And the forces of the universe
> To mechanize those wheels.
> His engines pulsed with power,
> He demanded roadways leading to
> The places he desired to go.

"I want a shorter road,
A faster road, a smoother road,
From my door
To the uttermost parts of the earth."

Ribbons of concrete spread
East and west and north and south,
Covered grasslands, gouged through forests,
Swallowed swamps and crippled marshes,
Paved the good black earth of fertile fields.
Concrete . . . pouring . . . pouring . . . pouring . . . ,
Burying ground two acres a minute.

Man destroys the source of his life
To get somewhere other than where he is.
More roads invite more cars to travel them,
Leading to more congestion,
Hastening the depletion of nature's stores,
The pollution of earth's air,
Destroying places where green things grow.

Will man become a wanderer upon his highways,
Because his roads have swallowed up his destination
Along with his place of departure?
Will he be doomed to travel to and fro
Until his engine stalls for want of fuel
And he draws one last poisoned breath?

I sincerely hoped that roads would not eat away any more of our seclusion here on the lake. I distributed my gear about my person again, pulled the folded jacket through my camera bag strap and stuck my hat on my head, then picked up the red hiking bag with my lunch in it. I was sure I would not make it around the lake without the lunch.

I could forget roads for a while. The ground sloped gently down to the next low area. I walked on a cushion of mosses and

81

grasses, with leathery trailing arbutus leaves twining through them to form a thick mat. On my first casual walks I had not even noticed the ground-hugging leaves.

As I became more observant, I realized that arbutus covers many of the lakefront areas, especially at this end. There is even a small bed at our boat landing. They bloom early, as soon as the snow melts, so I usually see only a few late blossoms among the brown withered ones. The blossoms are apt to be hidden under leaves, their own green ones and last year's discarded tree leaves. They are worth hunting for. Uncovering a few late white or pink waxy clusters of trailing arbutus is a thrill.

I hadn't quite believed the stories of their fragrance until I lay prone on the ground, my nose buried in them. Yes. The perfume was sweet enough and strong enough to overpower the familiar earthy smell of leaf mold and acid soil, and to make me forget about the exhaust fumes from cars. Someday I would see the trailing arbutus in full bloom. Just how heady would the scent of this whole slope of blossoms be? For now I had to be content with searching out the plump green buds in October to reassure myself the arbutus would be blooming in the spring, whether I saw and smelled it or not.

There are three possible routes at this point. In dry years I can take to the beach, a narrow strip of sand which takes me past the low spot in two or three minutes if I don't stop for botanizing. One extremely dry year I had followed the narrow animal paths right through the shrubs without getting my feet unduly wet. Usually I have to take time to walk around the well-defined perimeter. This was most surely the case today. There was no beach at all and water was well up into the bushes.

The circular area looked like an extension of the lake, a bay filled with vegetation. Very possibly it had once been a part of the lake. Now the leatherleaf has taken over, so I call it Cassandra Marsh. Each wet low area of the lake has its own characteristics, its own peculiar community of plants. This one was entirely shrubs.

A familiar birdsong sounded from the edge of the thickets, three staccato notes followed by a handful of golden notes tossed up to shower down like coins. Yes, song sparrows would be at home here, with shrubs and thickets and water. An extremely adaptable bird, the sparrow with a dark spot in the middle of its streaked breast is known all over the country in various habitats. This was his favorite.

The shrubs and water at our cabin lakefront attract song sparrows, too. Walking the deer path there one spring, I saw a sparrow scuttle quietly along the ground like a mouse, and disappear. I had seen this behavior before and guessed a bird slipped from its nest hoping I wouldn't notice. I found the nest right at my feet, in a hollow of the ridge made by a decaying log, with blueberry bushes and bracken masking the entrance. I peered in at the white eggs streaked with reddish brown, then left quickly, knowing there would be a waiting time before the bird would consider it safe to creep silently back to her brooding. I would not reveal the song sparrow's secret.

When there is no need for caution, sparrows sing all day and all season long from our lakefront shrubs and trees. I was aware of the variety of their song long before I read of it in books. There are normally three introductory notes, but following the announcement of identity, any combination of melody may follow. It ranges from the joyous "Maids, maids, maids, hang up your teakettle -ettle-ettle" which Thoreau heard, to the three mournful descending notes in a minor key that I hear persistently from our lakefront on overcast days. I have decided the song sparrow, so aptly named, has a song for every mood, and has as many moods as I.

The song sparrow in the Cassandra Marsh was sticking to tradition at the moment, tunefully calling maids to hang their teakettles and join him in song. I took it as an invitation to explore the bog.

The summer I followed the animal trail through, I had found that the leatherleaf, or Cassandra, forms a solid knee-high mass ringed by a variety of taller shrubs dominated by alders. Leatherleaf is a descriptive name, since the leaves are tough and durable enough to survive winter, but I prefer the more pleasant-sounding name, Cassandra. Especially when the shrubs are in bloom with their curving racemes of tiny white bells.

Cassandra is a name from Greek mythology, and Cassandra's story, when I looked it up, was gruesome. I was willing to accept Virginia Eifert's discreet version in her book *Journeys in Green Places*. Cassandra, according to Virginia, had a gift of prophecy, but Apollo forbade anyone believing her. Leatherleaf in the mass gives the effect of solid ground, but you'd better not believe it if you want to keep your feet dry, because Cassandra's feet grow in very wet places.

We see large expanses of these shrubs of uniform height as we drive area roads, and know they mean swampy ground. Many wetlands are left in Hiawatha Forest, and even more in the Manistique River Forest to the east, where maps indicate mile after mile of swampland.

The Seney Wildlife Refuge has been created in a part of the Manistique Swamp to provide an improved habitat for Canada geese, sandhill cranes and a variety of other wildlife.

"Yours is a goose lake," Arch told us when we built our cabin. The huge black and white Canada geese fly over in V-shaped flocks when the weather grows colder, announcing the coming of winter. Some years we are lucky enough to save three days for the October northwoods. Often we hear a noisy clamor as we gather around the cabin fire of an evening, and know geese are using our lake as an overnight stop. But it is always too dark to see them. We are wakened in the morning by their noisy early departure and can only listen to their voices fade away over the forest, southward.

At the Seney Refuge we can really observe Canada geese. The earth has been rearranged to form ponds where water levels can be controlled. In spring the water is kept deep enough to protect the nests on small secluded islands from predators. Then when goslings need food, the levels are lowered to expose the shallow feeding grounds of wild celery and bulrushes planted for that purpose.

A resident flock was established at the Refuge by clipping their wings. Their goslings flew south in the fall, along with wild flocks, to return "home" in the spring. These geese attracted other migrating flocks and a part of the swamp had truly become a refuge.

At home in the Midwest, such swamp and marshy areas have long since been drained for agricultural use, though in many fields it is still necessary to have an extensive system of drainage tiles to keep them that way.

Alders seem to be appointed guardians of most wet places, forming an outer barrier, as they did here around Cassandra Marsh. They are taller than I by several feet, their multiple trunks stiff and unbending and difficult to penetrate. I am always exhausted by the time I struggle through.

I would be content today just to walk around them. There were clusters of sweet gale outside the alder ring, as well as an occasional willow. More willows grow at the lakefront. At the end of May, two months ago, water had invaded the outer ring, making the grass soggy where I walked, reaching almost to a Juneberry bush in full bloom. Water now seemed confined to the bog center.

I swished through bracken as I walked around to the far side of the swamp. But what was this? Wheel tracks, even here? I had certainly intersected someone's trail. I followed it back in the direction I had come. The tracks led directly over hill and hollow to join the road to the campsite I had just left.

Indignantly I stomped back, following the tracks around Cassandra Marsh, to find a littered area of crushed grass at the very edge of what I thought was a secluded niche of the forest. Plastic bags and papers blew about and the tracks led on. As I suspected, they joined the road to the campsites across the lake from our cabin. Another part of my forest had been invaded. One more link in the network of roads around our lake had been forged, one more wild area had been exposed to civilization.

I walked on to the lake and stood looking back along the shoreline of Cassandra Marsh at the variety of shrubs at the lake edge. I bruised a leaf with my fingers and was rewarded with the pungent odor of aromatic sweet gale. The red osier was ordinary looking at this season, now that its brilliant spring stems were clothed in leaves. It is a rather poor cousin of the dogwoods, with insignificant white blooms, but the show of winter color makes up for it.

The winterberry, or Michigan holly, is very modest in summer, too. I looked in vain, trying to find the shrubs among the Cassandra, even though I thought I knew exactly where they grew. In late fall you can't miss them with their clusters of bright berries and leaves still green when other shrubs are naked. They too like wet areas. I had found their red berries at the mouth of the inlet stream, on the banks of the outlet stream and the inner shoreline of the shallow bay ahead of me.

The chokeberry bushes growing at the edge, hanging over the beach when there is one, were also indistinguishable now in the solid mass of green. In autumn some of their leaves turn a flaming red while others remain bright green, making a gay border which is even more interesting when their dark, plump berries are reflected in the lake. I first met chokeberries at our

86

cabin lakefront one June when their attractive buds and blossoms caught my eyes. They grow just a few feet from our boat landing, and song sparrows flit about their roots, especially at sunset.

The sprays of white bells of the Cassandra, scarlet holly berries, brilliant red osier shoots—what a display they would make if all were here at the same time! Again, nature is discreet in spreading the show the year round. I left Cassandra Marsh basking in the sun, turning my back on it to continue along the lake.

Sunlit Woods

I ignored the road as long as I could. As I walked over a log brilliant with green moss, I stooped to use the hand lens that dangled from a buttonhole. Tiny dots in the moss became striated fringed mushroom caps on fragile stems.

The miniature caps were tan to the naked eye, but magnified ten times they were a soft peach color, so delicate I hardly dared breathe for fear they would disintegrate. I placed them in the genus Mycena, but since my Mycena book back at the cabin was several inches thick, I wouldn't spend hours pinning down the particular species.

Looking the length of the log I found the pointed end of an old beaver cutting. Perhaps this was the tree we'd seen a lone beaver carrying branches from late one fall. He had industriously towed them across this end of the lake to the mouth of the inlet stream. At fishing time Fred and I investigated by boat and found a few branches piled on one bank.

"Probably a rogue beaver," Bob said when we told him about it. "A lone male roving around." Sure enough, by spring there was no sign of beavers, and high spring water had washed away the beginnings of his dam.

"This isn't getting me around the lake very fast," I thought, shading my eyes to look at the sun. It was nearly overhead. I walked back into the open grassy woods where walking was easier than through the lakefront growth. The pine, birch and aspen were scattered here, none of any great height. Bracken was thick under them in some places, grass in others.

I returned reluctantly to wheel tracks when I reached the first campsite on the south shore of the lake. Housetrailers sometimes sat here. It would be pleasant to live for a while in this secluded spot. There was no sign of wear and tear. Most people didn't bother to come to what had been the end of the tracks but stopped in more accessible sites.

I walked over to the path to the lake. A heavier cover of vegetation and less frequent use had protected the path from erosion by descending and ascending feet. Roots held the sand in place and the path, though visible, was a pleasantly natural one.

The next camping site, a bit farther down the lake, had been in use before we arrived in the woods. A makeshift, weather-worn table was pulled to one side, grass was worn away from the center, around the ashes of a fire. The area was large enough to include a complete traffic circle. The path to the lake was the sandy gash I had seen from my rest stop. The bank had eroded back into the campsite in a large semicircle. This must be the sandy scar we could see from our own side of the lake.

As I walked over to inspect the path, I saw that log steps were imbedded in the sand at convenient intervals down the slope. Each one held the sand of that step in place and stopped the erosion. It must have been a project of the Youth Conservation Corps. The Corps gives young people employment in the summer, an education in ecology and a means of improving our forest all at the same time.

As I turned from the steps, the picture of a bright red tomato caught my eye. Garbage had been put into a pit so shallow that if it had been covered at all, rain exposed it again. Cans of several kinds—potato salad, Campbell's soup, tomato juice, large Chef Boyardee, draft beer—and a plastic egg carton made up the unsightly mess. I could read the menu clearly. The sun highlighted the assorted trash.

89

Last fall when I had walked along here I spied something shiny back in the woods. Fall leaves were still bright, but enough had fallen to make the woods more open and to reveal, as I walked closer, a pine tree hung with discarded containers.

Back away from the campsite, hidden in summer, someone had indulged in a weird sense of humor. I wanted to apologize to the tree. A two-gallon peanut oil can dominated the decorations, with other empty cans and bottles stuck on branches higher than my head. Children could not reach that high, and ladders weren't usually part of camping equipment. Adults must have been responsible.

I didn't remove the trash. The Forest Service would be checking campsites and I wanted them to see this. The tree was rather symbolic of civilization, I thought, natural beauty obscured by man's discards. What an unpleasant subject to be reminded of in the woods.

> Garbage, Ugh!
> Grind it up,
> Flush it down the drain,
> Haul it away,
> Burn it, bury it.
> Anything to get it
> Out of my sight,
> Out of my mind.

Don't flush it into any water system that's going to
Return it through my pipes, into my faucet.
Don't dump it where I can smell it.
Don't burn it where it will pollute the air I'm
    breathing.
Don't bury it in my yard or my neighbor's.
Don't ruin the scenery I want to enjoy.
Don't pollute my water, air or soil.

There's no way to get rid of it?
   Just send it somewhere else.
Where on earth to put it?
   Well, surely there's someplace on earth. . . .
Oh. I see. Garbage really is here to stay . . .
   Here on earth.

I walked back into the woods to check on the garbage-hung tree. All was restored to its natural state. I wasn't even sure now which pine tree had been decorated. Garbage isn't usually that easily disposed of.

The Forest Service used to provide dumps for forest residents. We were kept informed about the one in current use and threw our refuse of all kinds into a deep trench which was periodically covered, then another opened. These dumps, unsightly and odorous as they were, provided entertainment. They attracted bears who came nightly to forage for food. In vacation season a line of cars rimmed the site at dusk. We watched a bear and cub one night, as the mother directed her offspring's activities. A sudden voice or arrival of another car, and the cub disappeared at signal from mother.

Even though I was curious about bears, I did not enjoy seeing them in this degrading situation. I wanted to see a bear in its natural habitat. A dump experience almost cured me of wanting to see them at all. One year when the dump had been moved much closer to our cabin, a friend and I drove in to leave our accumulation of garbage. Refuse was strewn all through the woods as we approached. Bears dragged the plastic garbage bags off into the woods to explore and scatter their contents at leisure.

My friend stopped her small car at the edge of the dump. There right before us in the heaped trench was the biggest bear I had ever seen. I guessed he was a grizzled old male. He turned his massive head to look straight at us, from ten feet away. I thought his eyes gleamed malevolently, though likely he was only peering nearsightedly.

"Are *you* going to leave the garbage?" my friend asked.

"N-no. I'm not getting out of this car," I quavered. The bear showed no signs of leaving his feast. We finally rolled down the window on the far side of the car and tossed our paper bag as far as we could. We didn't stay to do any bear watching, with that monster watching us. We had the feeling he could send our small car tumbling with one swipe of a paw.

Somehow I have not been as anxious to see a bear in the woods since then. Nor do I really regret not seeing the owner of the huge tracks we found in the late April snow right under our cabin windows one morning. I would not want to come face to face with that bear around the corner of our cabin.

The Forest Service has now eliminated this unnatural accumulation of bears at open dumps. Bears should search for their own natural foods and not become objects of entertainment for vacationers. Neat green garbage receptacles with heavily latched doors are located at collection points along forest roads for the use of residents, campers, travelers, fishermen and hunters. Garbage is collected regularly and taken to a central sanitary fill.

Sometimes they overflow after a holiday weekend, and the refuse is unsightly. The shed-sized green cubes are not exactly an aesthetic addition to the landscape at any time, but I realize they need to be visible and accessible. Garbage is unlovely, its disposal one of the crucial puzzling problems of our day, no matter where we are.

I shifted the camera strap on my shoulder to a less bony place. I didn't have my jacket for cushion now. I brushed through sweet fern bushes, bruising their leaves intentionally as I walked, to release their aromatic scent. Their fragrance was an effective antidote to the subject of garbage. I seemed to be the only one who paid much attention to the shrubs. Arch didn't even have a name for them when I had asked him about them.

They are not ferns at all, but shrubs, very twiggy ones at that, growing from eighteen to twenty-four inches high. Their leaves, however, are long and lobed and fern-like. Related to the sweet gale, they too owe their spicy scent to the bayberry family. But where the sweet gale grows in and near wet places, sweet fern likes dry sandy ones, such as Michigan's pine country. It is at home here in the open sandy woods and meadows.

I soon learned that the fragrance of sweet fern leaves is not only preserved in drying, but seems to grow stronger and sweeter. I sometimes gather a few leaves to take home to scent dresser drawers in the winter. One Christmas I stuffed tiny organdy sachets with them to include a bit of the northwoods in Christmas packages.

Burning sweet fern leaves make a good smudge to repel mosquitoes, I read, which is the most pleasant mosquito-repellent I can think of. I learned that the leaves have also been used as a substitute for tobacco. I think I might start a campaign among pipe smokers I know. I would happily inhale sweet fern smoke, especially if it keeps mosquitoes away at the same time.

The scent of sweet fern is more subtle than the balm of Gilead. You are aware of it on a sunny day when you pick blueberries in open places, when the heat of the sun releases the odor of its spicy resin, or as you brush its branches in reaching for berries.

Fred and I observed a ritual in early years as we arrived in the northwoods and turned off the highway into the sandy ruts of our road. Since we usually left home after Sunday church services, we arrived in the dark. We rolled down the car windows and inhaled deeply. When a sunny day had been followed by a light shower, all the scents of the northwoods were combined in a heady fragrance. I always thought I could detect the odor of sweet fern in this delightful welcome.

Back on the wheel tracks, I walked swiftly. It was time for a lunch stop, to refresh and refuel. To my left the ground sloped down to another low lakefront area that seemed impassable. Shrubs and small trees filled the understory. Someday I would take time to explore it.

As I came to the swimming beach area, I was relieved to find it unoccupied and neat. This had been a favorite camping and boat launching site for many years. The bank is just high enough for me to sit with my back to a tree or a stump and rest my feet on the beach.

One hot noon I had added a swift hike to the mailbox to my usual lake jaunt, and sat here gratefully, cooling my feet in the lake while I ate my lunch. A crawdad jumped into the water. A dragonfly hovered, and off in the shallows somewhere a frog went "Churrunk." It must have been early June, because I also remember the sweet spicy odor of balm of Gilead leaves on the breeze, an oriole singing in the top of the tree I leaned against. I sat enjoying cool feet, fragrant air, food, music and the panorama of the lake spread before my eyes.

When we were first on the lake people camped whenever and wherever they chose. The Forest Service had no designated campsites here. Then one year the house-shaped bulletin board on a brown post was in the area, with a garbage can beside it.

I remembered this because I had stood reading the regulations, and then raised my eyes to notice I could look directly at our beach across the lake. I had the whimsical idea of posting some suggestions of my own: "You are looking directly at Fred and Olive's beach. No loud noises or hilarious campfires. Use of binoculars prohibited. Fish on your own side of the lake. But make way for our boat in the pike hole over here. No camping in August, please. That is when we want to be in the woods." Selfishness dies hard.

We rarely have contact with the campers. I do my hiking

when sites are empty. But one year Fred on his way back from the mailbox met a fellow-preacher out gathering wood. He and his wife and four children were camped in this spot where I was now eating my lunch. Fred and I accepted their invitation to visit. To our amazement, we found the family housed in three pup tents. If you could call that "housed." The only other shelter was the family car, which had brought them and all their equipment. The children ranged in age from two years to early teens.

Theirs was really primitive camping. The family did all the cooking over the campfire. Water for drinking and cooking had to be carried from improved campsites several miles away. It began to rain while Fred and I sat on chunks of wood around their fire. Teenagers ran for the car, a sheet of plastic was shared and held over the heads of guests. The small children took refuge in the pup tents, heads sticking out so they wouldn't miss anything.

The family camped for two weeks in this simple fashion and seemed to enjoy every minute of it. Their only expense besides food was for a canoe they rented from an area resort. Somehow I could share my lake more happily with them in their obvious enjoyment of it than with the parties with elaborate camps and expensive equipment. This was real family togetherness, sharing camp chores which must consume a good part of their day, and enjoying one another's company.

"We'll see you next year," they promised as Fred and I pushed our boat out and started the motor to return to our cabin across the lake. "We're coming back!"

Eating my sandwich in the family's camping spot now, I remembered they had told about finding fresh stumps of small birch and aspen trees nearby. The trees evidently had been raided for camp use in good "living-off-the-woods" survival handbook fashion. Camping here is hardly a survival situation, unless it is the survival of the forest at stake.

I asked the district ranger, Pete, about regulations and he said, "The same rules are in effect here as at improved sites." Among other things, this means removal of all discarded materials from the site or placing them in containers that are provided. It also prohibits destruction, defacing or removing of any natural feature or plant. The rules are there to insure the survival of the forest, but they are no good unless people obey them.

"Do you have a record of people who use the campsites?" I asked the ranger.

"Each party is supposed to get permission from my office. The campsite permits are free, but this helps us regulate the use of them. Stay at any one site is limited to fourteen days for each party."

"The lake was certainly busy last weekend. It seemed every site was full of campers," I said.

"We limit the number of permits on your lake to six at a time," Ranger Pete told me. "We think that's the maximum it can accommodate without doing permanent damage."

"Of course, that means there is no damage if no one leaves garbage and junk around, if they don't cut trees or camp without permission," I thought. I read that in the Quetico-Superior Forest supplies have to be carried in burnable containers so there'll be no cans, bottles or foil to litter.

Some campsites there, according to the officials, had become "bald knobs" from misuse by the public. Dozens of trees were felled around one camp, evidently in a chopping contest, and around another to make an open space to discourage mosquitoes. I read a camping tip, in an outdoor magazine which had an ardent editorial on conservation, advocating cutting fresh pine boughs to place before the tent for a door mat, to keep the floor of the tent clean!

It isn't the use of nature, but the misuse of it that is destructive. The earth can grow new grass next spring to clothe trampled campsites, but it cannot grow new trees or tree limbs for each season's campers.

"Oh, those clouds," I exclaimed aloud, setting my lunch sack aside to reach for my camera. White clouds were massed dramatically against the blue sky, constantly changing shape, and repeated in the lake.

The shoreline curved out from the left, giving an interesting foreground for lake pictures at any time. I recalled one I'd taken from this very spot on a chill sunless day in mid-October. Many trees and shrubs were bare, but two birch trees opposite me still held on to some of their colorful leaves. When a gust of wind caught them, golden leaves showered down into the lake. The mood was somber, brooding and peaceful. I called the slide "Requiem for a Season."

As I looked through the viewfinder, I noticed that those same birches were now white skeletons against the sky, reaching up above the new green Cassandra growth. The consistently higher lake levels of recent years must have flooded their habitat. Birches do not like wet feet, but Cassandra shrubs do. "I must not blame man for all the changes around the lake," I reminded myself.

Woodcocks And Orioles

For the rest of the south shore from here to the outlet stream at the east end of the lake, I was on my own. I could leave man behind for a while as I struck out into the pathless area ahead of me. This part is too low and wet, overgrown and inaccessible for camping or picnicking. Or roads. So far no one has thought of a reason for one. If they do, it will mean our lake will be completely encircled by them. I have no regular route through, but simply walk where it is dry enough.

Fred's favorite pike hole in early years was a weed bed off this shore, so I was familiar with this part of the woods long before I explored it on foot. Fred would fish for perch for a while, then move into a deeper hole, using the perch for bait. I always brought my binoculars along. From our own beach across the lake we often saw deer coming down at dusk to drink here.

The blue heron was apt to flap up from somewhere back in the reeds and cattails to cross the lake as we watched, to land for a while in the treetops. I remembered the night I saw one in the very tip of a lakefront pine, a symbol of wildness as I walked alone in the rain. Finally the heron had flown off across the forest for the night.

On a spring day, while our boat floated over the pike hole, fishing was so slow that Fred decided we might as well look in the woods for morels. We didn't bother to start the motor, just pulled in his lines and rowed the short distance to shore.

98

"I'll pull the boat up and you can jump," he said, splashing overboard in his fishing boots.

I clutched my binoculars so they wouldn't bounce and jumped across the stretch of shallow water. "Oh, well, what's a wet foot . . . or two," I said, laughing, as I landed in sand so wet that water immediately made pools around my feet. We stepped up through prickly wild rose bushes to the bank.

"Those hardwoods back there look like a good place to start hunting mushrooms," Fred said, heading toward them. Then he found he had to detour around a thicket full of standing water.

Hiking in this area, as in dense forest, is not done in a straight line even though you might look at an open space and set a course directly across it. In the grassy places which we crossed on the way toward the trees, green was just beginning to show through last year's vegetation. There are twigs and small branches hidden there to trip you, or old stumps, wet hollows and long-fallen trees to detour around.

Suddenly right at our feet there was a flurry of wings. Feathers exploded into motion. A bird smaller than a partridge flew off to our left, not far from the ground, then disappeared into an alder thicket. We looked down. Right at the tip of Fred's boot were three brownish, mottled eggs in a shallow depression in the dead grasses.

"Did you see what it was?" I asked Fred, whose eyes are sharper than mine, especially when identifying moving objects.

"I know it wasn't a killdeer," Fred said. We had found just such a shallow nest on the sandy beach, and the killdeer had run and flown ahead of us, tolling us away from the nest.

"I thought I saw a flash of orange as it flew," I said. "Let's mark the spot and leave quickly so the bird will come back. If we can get that close before she leaves the nest, I should be able to get a picture of her on it."

"These sticks form an angle here," Fred said.

"Yes. I've noticed killdeer nests, too, are apt to be near them. Do you suppose they are a protection of a kind? Or do birds need markers, too?"

Fred retraced his steps. "This stump with blueberries around it would be easy for you to remember. Why don't you come sight the angle of the nest from here. I'll keep my eye on the spot."

"That should be simple," I said as I joined him and marked the place he pointed out. "I wonder if it isn't a woodcock?"

"Is that the dumpy-looking bird we saw in our yard at home early one spring?"

"Yes. It looked like it was all bill," I said, laughing. "We saw that one sitting, and this one flying. I will have to check my bird book."

We walked away from the nest and the lake back into maple and aspen woods. The maple leaves were mostly green, with a few reddish tints left for color. The aspens were just leafing out, giving an open look to the woods. The effect was of silver mist, I thought.

"Isn't it lovely?" I asked, looking toward the lake. Fred had been watching the ground for morels.

He glanced up, then said, "Look. A deer!"

"Where?" I asked breathlessly.

"Way over there, moving across that open glade down near the lake," Fred said, pointing.

"Oh-h-h. That makes it perfect," I said softly, as the tawny deer moved leisurely across the glade and with a flick of its white tail was gone.

We didn't find any morels, but Fred caught a keeper pike as we trolled home in the boat. While the water heated for dishes and Fred cleaned his fish, I checked on woodcocks. Sure enough. They do have orange coloring which shows in flight. And their eggs are mottled and tannish.

100

I walked around the lake with my camera the next evening while Fred fished the pike hole. I found the stump, sighted the direction of the nest and approached cautiously. It was near that arrangement of twigs. No. I must be mistaken. Nothing there. I took another step, looking for landmarks. There was a startling explosion of feathers at my feet once again, and once again I was looking at the nest of eggs.

I tried on another day but I still could not spot the woodcock before it flew. I decided to take a picture of the eggs and gave up trying to get the bird, too. I didn't want to bother the woodcock again.

One spring as Rita and I drove along the entrance road on our arrival late in the afternoon, Rita braked suddenly just past the culvert over the outlet stream.

"Look," she said, pointing to the road ahead.

"A woodcock. Can you believe it?" I asked, laughing.

The awkward-looking bird with bill so long and heavy it seemed about to tip him over moved to the side of the road and disappeared. We had barely gotten under way again when a larger woodcock appeared in the road ahead of the car. As it crossed to the side of the road, we saw two immature birds, copies of their comical parents.

The adult bird proceeded to lead the young back across the road so casually that Rita and I were able, with binoculars, to study the intricate camouflage patterns of the feathers on their squat bodies. The pattern seemed to be completely random, and yet it was a definite mottling, not just a mixture of brown, beige and white feathers. The woodcocks were oblivious of observers. They walked through the sweet fern and blueberry bushes at a leisurely pace, then disappeared in a nearby thicket.

"Now that's what I call a fitting introduction to your woods," Rita said with a satisfied sigh. "Nicer than the skunk we saw back there."

101

I have learned since that the long stout beak is used for probing mud for the worms and grubs that are the mainstay of the woodcock's diet. And no wonder I had not been able to see the bird at my feet, with the patterned back resembling twigs, dead leaves and grass, lichens and moist bare ground.

The woodcock's famous mating serenade, when the male ascends spirally, high into the air, releasing his shower of tinkly song as he descends again, occurred before our first spring trips. One year I was at the cabin in early May. The area in which I'd seen woodcocks as well as their nests has an open area nearby which seemed a likely setting for the serenade. I could easily walk around to it at sunset time, but coming back in the dark was to risk a sprained ankle or a broken leg. The outlet stream culvert where Rita and I had seen the woodcock family was my next choice. It could be reached by road and traveled safely after dark with a flashlight.

When I came to the grassy place I had mentally pictured, I found it not nearly as open as I had remembered. Small aspens were encroaching. But surely it was large enough. I found a spot where I had a good view, a tree trunk for a backrest, and settled down to wait. The sun was just setting.

As the sound of my footsteps, then my scrunching about to find a comfortable position, died away, I expected silence. Instead I heard "closing of day" sounds all around me—scraps of birdsong, a variety of contented chirps, rustlings and scratchings, the "glub-glub" of a frog over in the pond. But no courting woodcocks. Perhaps it was too early. A whitethroat piped its high sweet notes far away.

There was a glow behind the trees I faced. The moon was coming up. I realized I had been hearing some persistent scratching sounds. They seemed to come from the backlighted treetops. I tipped my head back. There was a dark shape in a crotch of the tallest pine.

Was it a bear cub? I looked around uneasily, then used my binoculars. Could be. If so, I had better be somewhere else quickly. I remembered the time twin cubs crossed in front of our car, and I had to forcibly restrain my friend from jumping out with her camera. Where there are cubs there is a mother bear who is notoriously short-tempered where her young are concerned.

The dark shape moved. I heard a crunching sound. My binoculars showed a bare patch on the trunk, a small head protruding from a round body. I relaxed. A fat old porcupine was waking up for breakfast after a day in the treetops. It slowly worked its way down the tree from branch to branch, often stopping to crunch on bark. The moon slowly rose behind the porcupine's tree until the clearing was filled with moonlight. And moonlight only. I was going to hear no woodcocks, but could their song be any more stirring than a white-throated sparrow singing in the forest dusk? I didn't need my flashlight after all. The moon lighted my way back to the cabin. The woodcock serenade is one adventure still awaiting me.

"Woodcocks prefer moist thickets," I affirmed now, remembering my bird book. That description certainly fit this area I was hiking, as well as the outlet stream where I had seen a porcupine instead. In fact the nesting site was under water now and I could not walk where it had been. There is a dry ridge along the bank at the lakefront which I could follow this time.

To my left as I walked was a waist-high border of wild roses, joe-pye weed and turtlehead. The ridge was only a few feet wide. I had to watch my footing so I wouldn't slip down into the shallow water and mud on the other side, or walk into an overhanging alder that would knock off my hat.

I soon came out into a grassy glade which I always remember in sunlight. There was the sunlight of the spring day Anna and I had taken a leisurely rest stop here, serenaded by an oriole which moved from one treetop to another, brighter than the sun. His jubilant trilling came from one direction, then another, a whole chorus of orioles all by himself.

"I think he's trying out the acoustics," Anna said, chuckling.

In the sunlight of a fall day a flock of myrtle warblers had cheerfully fluttered in and out of the small trees as I slowly walked across this clearing by myself, without Anna to say, "Let's stop." I stood still occasionally to train my binoculars on the yellow flashes of color on the dark birds as they kept just ahead of me. They were cheerful company all down the lakefront. I could see their yellow rumps, and remembered that practical ornithologists have renamed the myrtle warbler the "yellow-rumped warbler."

The cedar waxwings here today did not seem to mind my presence. I was able to get close enough to see their wing feathers with their scarlet "sealing wax" tips, which give them their name. I like the description in the guidebook by Henry Hill Collins, Jr.: "Waxwings have a sedate upright posture and are gentle, tame and gluttonous." I prefer this to the long lyrical description of their coloring in a large birdbook I read. I saw them with crested heads, coppery brown coloring with tailored touches of black, yellow and white.

Small chokecherry trees dotted the clearing. The birds were likely attracted to their fruit. At home flocks of waxwings light in a cedar tree and strip off its blue berries. A high-bush cranberry has scarlet fruit all winter unless a flock of the birds find it and leave it bare. No one could deny that these handsome birds are gluttonous. Overripe berries in quantities sometimes make them behave as if intoxicated. On the other side of the ledger they are just as gluttonous in attacking the harmful worms or insects that infest trees.

Bird-watching wasn't getting me around the lake. I moved on into the shadier woods carpeted with bracken. Beneath the bracken fronds was yet another carpet. The three- or four-inch evergreen "cedars" of the club moss family grow along with the ground "pines" at various places, including our cabin lot, but this was the densest, most picturesque patch of them that I had found around the lake.

Wintergreen flourishes here too, and berries are plentiful enough most years that there are enough to feed wildlife and leave a few to delight my eyes as I walk by. In late May or early June this is a gaywings garden. The vibrant purple of the miniature trumpets of the tiny fringed milkwort, as it is also called, adds more color to the ground-hugging evergreen garden. The gaywings plants are so inconspicuous that you only know they are there when they bloom.

This would be a good place to say dramatically to a companion, "This is the Canadian carpet!" The low-growing persistent mat of vegetation would never be any taller. It would not shoot up into impenetrable tangles of rank growth as does the undergrowth in the woods at home in the Middle West. Or as tropical jungles do.

By the time the earliest spring flowers have bloomed you might as well forget walking in Illinois woods that are in a natural ungrazed state. My first impression of the northwoods had been the openness of it. This meant, to my delight, that I could explore all summer long. I could thank the Ice Age for this opportunity, at least for the delightful, mostly evergreen combination of low plants which the glacier, dipping down into my country, had brought from Canada. There are reminders of it all around the lake.

> It is good that I am reminded
> Of immeasurable time,
> Of eras stretching back into a void as endless
> As the black spaces of the universe reaching out.
> Stretch my mind, O Lord, to the limits of elasticity.
> Pry it out of a mold that is aware only of
> The infinitessimal flash of my lifetime,
> Of the microscopic world I inhabit.
> Sling it out into space to watch the world revolve,
> Out into the ages and eons of time

To see the changing contours, the flux of land and sea,
The turbulent air, blowing hot then cold,
The uneasy crust, the molten core.
Then before I am lost out there in the stars,
Catapult me back to the earth I walk,
To the time I know,
With a mind pliable enough, wondering enough,
To worthily inhabit my small niche
And to give to you, the Mastermind of it all,
God of the universe and of me,
God of the ages and of the moment,
All honor and glory forever and ever,
Time and space without end,
Amen and amen.

I walked on. "Yes, Lord. Stretch my mind till it hurts." And it
will hurt if I am to break out of the shell of self.

Willow Swales

Ahead of me now a solid barrier of alders surrounded another wet area. This was no Cassandra Marsh to walk through in bright sunlight when it was dry enough. Branches closed overhead and it was dark, gloomy and forbidding looking.

Because I had been here in leafless spring, I knew I could follow the shoreline for a short distance if I wanted to struggle through. I would be on a narrow peninsula that extended in a thin line of vegetation, paralleling the indented shoreline for some distance, forming a long shallow hidden bay.

The bay had given me a memorable misty morning. The lake was shrouded in a light airy fog as I carried my Pyrawa from the cabin to the lake and tossed it in. The air was almost luminous, and I hurried for fear the sun and breeze would clear it. Sitting in a boat on the mist-shrouded lake had been a passion with me since my first experience years ago. Fred told me how delightful it was fishing on the lake in the pre-dawn hours. One morning I had joined him, stumbling down the path in the half light, a heavy jacket warming my back but not my icy fingers. Drifting entranced, I experienced a moment of high exhaltation.

Preparing to relive that moment, I pulled my air-filled boat next to Fred's steel one and stepped in. In my haste I forgot. There I was again, sitting in the lake, with my boat floating alongside. I was wet from the waist down—jeans, long johns

107

and all, in a fifty-degree temperature. But I had a warm dry jacket. I stood up, plunked myself squarely into the middle of the boat and pulled my wet feet in after me. I wasn't going to waste the misty morning.

I paddled along the shoreline which I could just see as a darker shape to my left, until I guessed I might be in a line with the small break in the shrub barrier that formed the inlet. I then headed across the lake. When darker misty shapes materialized out of the nothingness that surrounded me, there was the opening. I had navigated on course without instruments or stars.

I entered the bay, rested my double-ended paddle across the boat, and drifted. There was not a sound. Dimly I could see bulrushes and cattails on three sides of me. Rushes scratched against the boat. I drifted into them and stopped. Silence again. Stretched from cattail blades ahead of me was a perfect spider web, outlined with dewdrops. I sat relaxed, my mind open and receptive, my spirit soaring, lifted on wings.

My husband would ask me what I was doing. For him the reason for going out on a misty morning like this is to catch fish. The atmosphere is only a pleasant setting for his real purpose. Fred preaches a practical religion to his congregations, and expects something to happen because of it. Faith produces works. He is fond of the story of the preacher who preached the same sermon Sunday after Sunday. When his congregation finally rebelled, he told them, "When I see some results from that sermon, I will preach another."

There is nothing monotonous about my husband's preaching. I did overhear a complaint one morning. One lady said to another as they went out of the church door, "He doesn't preach a very comfortable sermon, does he?" Fred was pleased when I reported the conversation. He likes to follow his sermon with the hymn, "Rise Up, O Men of God," sending his people out with a call to action.

108

This is one reason Fred needs our forest retreat, with a month or so out of the year away from the frustration of such high expectations. He is so often disappointed by those who want a "comfortable" religion. But with retirement this need would be gone. Already he has looked elsewhere for fishing. Where my roots had grown deep into this forest land of Hiawatha, his were letting go. I could happily make my home here. This dream had been shattered by my husband's firm declaration, "I want to live near people I know, where I can garden."

As I sat bemused with my own thoughts, there in the misty inlet, a slight breeze shook drops from the spider web. I became aware of a growing brightness. The sun was soon going to break through the mist. Such is the power of mind over matter that it wasn't until I extricated myself from the canoe back at our beach and stood again on land that I remembered my wet clothing. The layer of air surrounding me in the inflated canoe had been good insulation.

But that was another day. I was afoot now, and could see nothing of the bay through the dense border of alders surrounding the low wet area immediately back of the cattails. My usual path around it was the slope outside the alders. Anna and I had walked it one spring, discovering morels on the moist bank when our eyes became used to distinguishing them from dead leaves. We had finished our circuit of the thickets with muddy feet, enough of the choice mushrooms for a meal and a decided list to starboard from walking with one foot downhill from the other.

The many fallen logs on the slope made excellent hunting for bracket mushrooms of all kinds. I found it exciting to peer beneath the various sized shelves and ruffles for the pore surface beneath. It might turn out to be purple or red, brown or white. There might be knife-edged gills, a smooth surface, the mouths of spore-bearing tubes, teeth hanging down, or any combination of patterns and shapes. But I mustn't get involved

109

in that today, either. Mushrooms would prolong my lake exploration even more than bird-watching, since they stay put.

Like all the other low areas around the lake, this one varies from year to year and season to season. Today I would have to walk well out and around it the whole way, two or three times the actual distance. Water stood around the roots of the alders, even though it was past the middle of summer.

On a brisk sunny day in October I had peered through the forbidding alder barrier, stooping to look through the leafless area where the multiple dark trunks were massed like a stockade wall. The willow leaves and bark just beyond were light and sunny in comparison, and I could see no water. I could always retrace my steps if it got too wet.

I pulled my hat firmly onto my head, huddled into a compact mass, clutched my camera and hiking bag close to protect them, then backed through the most likely looking spot. I winced at the scratching scraping sounds, then, safely through, tried to straighten up. A tug stopped me halfway. One last alder branch had reached out for my binocular strap. I freed it and turned around into the willows. How welcoming they were with their soft leaves and pliable branches.

I had not tried to identify the many species of the willow family. These were shrubs six feet or more high, rounded in shape. I walked easily through the first ring of them and was surprised to come out into an open grassy glade. It was a small circular room, the cheerful light greens and yellows of the willows the walls, the blue sky a ceiling. Knee high, gracefully arching grasses made a shag carpet.

The carpet pad was black and oozy, but that was a small matter. As I looked down at my feet I realized there were other footprints. Under the grasses I could see a narrow churned black trail only a few inches wide, pocked with deer tracks. It led straight across the glade toward the hidden bay.

As I looked at the grasses again, the only evidence of the trail

110

was a faint riffle where the grass blades had been disturbed by the passing deer. Secret places, safe places, yet open to the sun, the sky, the wind.

> Holy of Holies,
> The secret place of the Most High,
> Overlaid with golden sunshine,
> Walled with willow draperies,
> Giving easy access to the seeker,
> Closing the way behind with
> Curtains of soft leaves,
> All open above,
> Access free, unhindered.
> Eyes are blinded
> That look upward too long,
> Dazzled by the glory.

> Tarry not.
> No mossy log, no place to rest,
> No sturdy trunk to lean against,
> Unwelcoming cold, wet earth.
> The path leads in . . . and out.
> Bow the head then and receive.
> Let his power fill you,
> Warm you through and through,
> And reverently depart.

As I passed from one small opening to another, I found deer trails in all. Deer can walk out into the cattails to drink by means of these delightful avenues, without being seen. The deer are here even though I rarely see them.

Biologists at the Cusino Wildlife Refuge a few miles north of us proved the prowess of deer at concealment when they put thirty-nine deer into a fenced enclosure a mile square and turned six veteran hunters loose to find them. Four days went

111

by before the men sighted one buck. In South Dakota a buck with orange streamers and radio attached evaded skilled observers for seven days, even with operators tuned in to his movements.

When I read that it was believed deer can detect a flicker of movement a half mile away, I marveled that I ever saw deer. Particularly when the deer are so silent themselves and capable of standing without a movement for hours. I try sometimes to walk quietly in the woods, and know as I listen to the noise I make that any wild creature, deer or deer mouse, has taken cover long before I arrive.

I cherished my rare experience with a deer one June evening. The mosquitoes and I had the woods to ourselves. Insect repellent kept bugs from being too friendly as I walked to the end of the lake to enjoy the sunset. Deer tracks pocked all the roads I walked, so I paid no special attention to the fresh tracks in the service road.

The clearing where the power line branches off across the forest is a choice mushroom hunting area, with stumps and logs strewn about. A large bleached stump usually holds a salt block put out by a nearby cabin owner. As I glanced into the clearing, a deer was looking at me from a few yards away. I froze, expecting it to leap away. The animal flicked its big ears. Then it casually went back to licking salt. I watched a while, then slowly raised my binoculars, expecting the deer to be gone by the time I looked through them.

I saw the velvety texture of developing antlers, patches in a rough hide, the outline of ribs. The buck raised his head again and looked curiously at me. There was a scar on his left shoulder. He lifted his left hind foot and scratched his black nose a couple of times. Mosquitoes were bothering him and he didn't have mosquito repellent to help. The deer moved to another stump and back again.

I waved my hand slowly. Still he showed only curiosity. I

112

gave a quick normal gesture of greeting. Still the buck showed no alarm but went on licking, occasionally lifting his head to observe me. I moved slowly on, watching the deer over my shoulder. When I resumed my normal walking pace, he finally lifted his white tail flag and bounded slowly off. I could still see him behind a screen of popple as I looked back. I had communed with the scarred old buck for a quarter of an hour. I would know him if I saw him again. Perhaps he had already seen me many times in these woods.

I had another excuse for not seeing deer. There are fewer deer in the area now. The herds are dwindling back to the size they were when white men first entered the country. I had to give up my romantic delusions of a forest primeval abounding in wildlife. Lumbering created brushlands where deer and other wild creatures flourished. The peak deer population of the Upper Peninsula was in the '30s and '40s because of the earlier timber cutting.

The shrinking population now is due to the increasing maturity of the forests. In a mature woods, browse grows out of reach of deer, and the floor is increasingly shaded and bare of new growth. Leaving forests to mature naturally means starving out the deer. The buck I had seen was certainly not an example of a sleek well-fed deer.

Again I was reminded that nature is never static. With my own eyes I know the forest is gaining. Open spaces that were prevalent along the entrance road are fast disappearing. Our own yardsticks are the young balsams near our cabin, one near a firecircle log, the other a few feet from our picture window.

The firecircle fir was about three feet high, a miniature Christmas tree under which we had put gifts for a childrens' birthday party the year we built. Adding a whorl of branches each year, the tip of it is now way beyond anyone's reach. The picture window fir was so frail and lopsided when we cleared the trees for the cabin that we ignored it, not expecting it to

113

live. Now it is a nicely shaped tree reaching above the eaves.

The forest is maturing. Deer are disappearing. And along with the deer we miss other wildlife that thrives in the same conditions. "Most birds and animals found in Michigan are creatures of the brush. They like deep forests as a place to scamper into . . . but they *live* in brush. That's where they find their food, that's where they find protection, and that's where they find each other," I read in Michigan's conservation magazine.

Should man let nature take its course? As reluctant as I am to find myself on the side of hunters and Big Business, I would like to see deer increase. But at the expense of the forest I live in? I finally got up enough courage to ask the ranger what is being done about it.

"Selective cutting, like that in our hardwoods. That will do the job, won't it?" I asked hopefully.

Ranger Pete shook his head. "Not a chance. A beaver might as well try to build a dam with one aspen twig." I could see him hesitating. "Probably he is sizing me up, wondering how frank he can be without incurring the wrath of a sentimental female," I thought.

"The public likes to think we are a bunch of busybodies who don't know what we are doing," he said.

"I am afraid I've been guilty myself," I said, smiling as I remembered my reaction to the lumbering within sight of our own cabin. "But I am beginning to see some of the problems involved and would really like to make a more intelligent approach."

"Well, in a nutshell it's this. The problem, as you have seen, is to open up the Forest. Congress so far has voted us only a pittance for wildlife management as such, but in Hiawatha Forest we consider the effect on wildlife when we plan our commercial timber cutting."

"What about state forests? Aren't they doing a lot of experimenting at the Cusino Refuge?"

"Some of the top experts in the country have been conducting studies of deer in relation to their environment there, and publishing their scientific findings in professional journals. Their recommendations are controlled burning, logging, supervised clear-cutting, bulldozing where there's no commercial value, to increase the areas more favorable to wildlife."

"Bulldozing! Clear-cutting!" I exploded before I could stop myself. "How awful!"

Ranger Pete grinned at me wryly. He's saying, "I knew she couldn't take it," I thought. In a few moments I managed to grin feebly back.

"But . . . how awful for people with cabins nearby."

"Naturally we don't do this in more public areas, because not many people would accept the explanation that they would eventually see more deer. As you know, the national forests are multipurpose areas, with three main goals: to produce a continuing wood supply, provide outdoor recreation for the public, and preserve wildlife. We are always being accused by one interest of favoring another."

"Whew! You do have a job, don't you?" I said fervently.

The first man
Who made a clearing in the forest,
A shelter from its trees,
Scratched a furrow with a stick
And dropped a seed,
Assumed dominion, his ordained place,
As one who manages creation,
His own bit of it, in his own way.

Four men in a hundred miles
Are a vastly different matter
Than four hundred men in one.
He who dams a stream
Denies one neighbor, floods another.
His refuse offends the eyes and nose of others.

115

His weeds blow seeds into adjoining fields,
His animals running free destroy the crops.
His dominion clashes with that of his brother.
Fences, laws, boundaries, names,
Zones, parks, preserves, deeds and regulations
Lead to lawsuits and to wars.
The more people there are,
The more the exercise of dominion affects another.

> Dominion, though God-given,
> Is no simple matter.
> We need knowledge of that domain,
> Wisdom in using what we know,
> Understanding of diverse needs.
> Above all, we must remember
> The Creator gives us dominion
> But not an outright deed.
> He is still Lord of all.

I made my circle of the hidden willow swales, remembering them, appreciating the experience all the more because I knew it to be a rare one. In the same way I savored the thought that there are mountains I will never climb, wilderness lakes I will never see. It is enough to know that they are there, that they belong to the Creator, in spite of man's claims.

Suddenly a grouse flew up as I approached the lake at the other side of the marshy area. I was reminded that it isn't only deer but all the wildlife associated with them that conservationists are concerned about. "What's good for deer is also good for grouse and snowshoe hares," they said.

"And also good forestry," Ranger Pete would add.

"The problem is," I thought, "do people know what's good for them?" The question echoed in my mind. "Do I know what's good for me?"

116

Popple, Aspen And Bam

Bracken ferns formed a continuous cover all the way around the marsh, scarcely reaching my knees at first. As I walked they grew taller and taller. When they reached my waist I had to hold my gear high to keep it from tangling in the fronds.

In the stand of dense aspen woods I was approaching there were two visible layers of green—the roof formed by aspen branches, and the understory one of bracken. The three large fronds of the fern grow at the top of a stout naked stem and are parallel to the ground. When Gladys and I hiked this area together, I had turned to tell her about the aspen woods in spring.

"Gladys?" I called, startled. My companion had completely disappeared. I heard a chuckle and saw an unnatural movement of bracken fronds.

"I'm down here, taking a picture of the sun shining through the fern roof," my friend reassured me.

I squatted down to peer beneath the fronds. I could see Gladys through the stems, aiming her camera skyward. "This is a whole world in itself down here, isn't it? Wildlife must love this cover," I said. Gladys mumbled a reply, intent on exposing her picture properly. I had already used all my film.

"Oh, look at those plump blueberries," I exclaimed. We often find choice berries under bracken. Gladys and I had been eating our way around the lake, snatching handfuls as we walked. There were blueberries on every bush that year, it seemed. Evidently the blossoms had escaped the usual late frost last spring, and abundant rainfall in July swelled every fruit. Gladys and I were cramming so much into the few days we had to explore together that berry-picking as such was not on the agenda.

"They're better this way anyway," Gladys said.

I vowed I had eaten my last handful. But these were as large as cultivated berries. I reached for the plumpest bluest berries and held them in my hand, admiring their frosty bloom before I popped them into my mouth. M-m-m. I stood up to relieve my cramped knees and was back in the upperstory world.

I wasn't pleased with the description of bracken in my dictionary. "Our only weedy fern," it said when I looked it up. Anything growing so profusely invites the label, I suppose, or anything growing in so many parts of the world. Mature woods are free of it, as are marshes and swamps, but everywhere else I walked in the area I found bracken.

In the driest open areas the plants are short. Books say they grow from eight to eighteen inches high. Here in a protected, moist place I was sure the stems were three feet tall. The bracken was tiring to walk through. Besides holding my gear above it, I could not see my feet to know whether my next step would throw me into a hole or over a log. I found I had to do more detouring around windfalls, climbing over and under debris in this area, anyway, where there were no established paths.

Bracken is rather a temporary part of the northwoods scene, I realized. When spring flowers bloom around the cabin, bracken sticks are just beginning to poke up through the ground. It is in the middle of June at least before they reach their full growth and make a thick carpet layer in our lakefront woods. Peering under bracken has become second nature to me. Before we leave the woods at the end of August, bracken

118

fern in the more explosed places has already turned brown and curled up its fronds. Bracken season is brief, two or three months at most.

Sheltered in the woods in the aspen grove, it persists later, and the fronds turn lovely shades of gold, umber and burnished bronze, forming a muted patterned background for the gaudy display of fall color. One autumn when we were disappointed on our brief three-day trip to find trees still green about the lake, the golden ferns beneath them with sun shining through compensated.

In dire extremity the bitter bracken roots have been ground and mixed with barley to ward off starvation. Evidently they aren't a very choice food. The leaves have astringent qualities and at one time were used in medicine and also in the process of dressing hides for leather. The dried fronds are used to bed cattle in some parts of the world. Gathering bracken hay would be a pleasant job, I thought as I read about it.

The large-toothed aspen trees rose out of the bracken in a solid stand. I put my hand on one of the trunks. The straight smooth boles had a golden tan bark with greenish undertones that gave the effect of sunshine whether the sun shone or not. I remembered a windy day in fall when their leaves were bright yellow and in constant motion, as is the manner of poplars. With the bracken beneath them a burnished gold, they made sunshine for the whole forest.

In earliest spring when the snow has just melted and the bracken is still dormant beneath the duff, this is another world. You can look up through bare branches to the sky, look long distances through open corridors, and see every detail of the forest floor. The openness then is in direct contrast to summer. As I stood there in the aspen grove I had the feeling I could be swallowed up in all the lush greenery of bracken and aspen with my cries for help muffled and unheard.

One year I walked these woods when they were still in their

open phase. Suddenly with no bracken to hide them I became aware of huge old stumps scattered through the maturing aspen woods. The largest of the aspens is no more than a dozen inches in diameter, and the blackened stumps loomed like giants. I tried to imagine the immense girth and height of the pine or hemlock trees that once grew here, the forest that the first landlooker and lumbermen knew.

I re-created that forest in my mind, sitting on the horizontal roots of one of the remnants, and heard the commotion of lumbering, the echoing of axe and saw, the shouts of sawyers and teamsters, the thud, crash and shaking of earth as one by one the trees fell. I saw a massive trunk swiftly chopped free of encumbering branches, then the team of horses straining to skid the massive log out of the snowy woods over an icy trail.

I saw the litter of slash stacked high over the denuded land, drying into tinder for the first flash of lightning to ignite into a roaring holocaust that destroyed everything in its path, including any seeds that might have re-created the forest. Only the blackened stumps were left. I saw aspen seeds drift in and take root around the stumps. Solid stands of sunny hardwoods eventually took the place of the dark green conifer giants that once completely dominated the gloomy needle-carpeted aisles beneath them the year round.

Ruffed grouse enjoy the openness of spring aspen woods. "If you want to find grouse in the spring, just look up in the aspen trees. That's where the birds will be, eating the buds," Ranger Pete told me.

The grouse are sometimes in the aspens in fall, too, during hunting season. Rita stopped the car suddenly one October day as we traveled the road past the outlet stream, not far from these woods. She pointed up through the windshield with one hand and fumbled for her camera with the other. There on an aspen branch, perched right over the road, was a ruffed grouse. We saw the silhouette of its small crested head and rounded

120

body as the bird walked about the branches, posing obligingly for our cameras.

As we left we passed the swamp road turnoff. Arch and a hunting buddy were sitting there in his truck, guns ready, trying to decide which way the "partridge," as they called the ruffed grouse, had gone. We smiled smug innocent smiles and did not enlighten them.

"Bird" season and the peak of fall color coincide. This is pleasant for hunters, but aggravating to me, especially when Fred and I have only three short days between Monday and Friday, our long weekends as we call them, to sample various seasons. On one of those days I listened from the cabin for shots, and took off in the opposite direction for my hike around the lake, wearing a red hat. I came back chuckling. I flushed grouse in the thickets around every swamp I circled. The birds seemingly had the same idea as I. The smart ones left the aspen trees and took refuge in thickets.

The first part of June is my favorite time to walk in the aspen woods. The large-toothed aspen is the last tree to leaf out, and as delicate infant leaves emerge from the buds they are covered with a soft white down that gives a frosty open look to the trees. You look up at the blue sky through a veil of silver lace. Since it is also warbler time in the northwoods, bright flashes of color enliven the scene. The small birds become temporary jewels in the lace. Because most other trees are in full leaf by then, aspen trees are the easiest place to bird-watch in June.

And then comes "aspen day," when the air is full of floating silken tufts of seeds from the long catkins drooping beneath the leaves. The tiny parachutes reflect sunlight as they drift, gather in piles of cotton on the ground and clog screens, a reminder that they are related to the cottonwoods.

It was summer now, and I walked out of the aspen woods into a miniature forest of twinkling little "popple" trees, the quaking aspen. They come up like weeds in clearings and burnt-

121

over ground, and grow like them too. Their small rounded leaves catch the sunlight as they twirl and dance on their fragile stems, set at right angles to the leaf blade.

Friends whose cabin is not deep in the woods, as ours is, had one year cleared the small quaking aspens from the grassy area between their cabin and the service road. It seemed that six popped up where one had been before, and already a quaking aspen forest nearly hid the cabin. The little poplars are short-lived trees, and I found few mature ones on the route of my lake hike.

I passed the popple and came to the lakefront, where there was a concentration of another poplar, the balm of Gilead tree. Rough bark makes them different from other poplars, as does the fact that they prefer wet places. The balm of Gilead trees are so ordinary in appearance that I long overlooked them, discovering the trees finally through the sense of smell. I traced a permeating fragrance in the spring woods, expecting to find a tree in full bloom. Instead I found sticky new leaves whose perfumed resin clung to my fingers as I carried a twig back to the cabin for identification.

The name "balm of Gilead" evidently belonged first to an Asian tree but was borrowed for the balsam poplar. I was intrigued by the association the name called up.

"Is there no balm in Gilead?" the woeful prophet Jeremiah wailed. "Is there no physician there?" From my childhood the words of a folk hymn faintly remembered answered a question I had not asked. Nor did I know then that Jeremiah had.

"There is no balm in Gilead to make the wounded whole." I found that authorities do not agree as to the tree which furnished this healing balm, some saying that it must have come from elsewhere and been exported by Gilead, which was a country on trade routes to Egypt. Others name a local tree as the source.

At any rate, the tree was immortalized by Jeremiah and an

122

American folk hymn. Arch said that locally the tree is known as "bamagilea." I had also heard the name "bamagilly," both evidently contractions. To lumbermen, Arch said, the tree is simply "bam."

When the wind blows from the south on a spring day, the fragrance is carried across the lake to the cabin area. The sticky resin coats the buds heavily, protecting them from winter cold, and adheres to the leaves as they develop. New leaves are shiny with it, and later the mature ones have brown splotches where it dries. I pressed my original specimen between the pages of my tree book, and even now the delightful scent is there when I open the book at home for winter study. Arch said pioneers boiled the buds down to make a salve from the balm.

I learned something else in studying the tree. If anyone had asked me what the word "balsam" meant, I would have replied, "A fir tree." I discovered it is an "aromatic, resinous substance with healing properties, produced by plants." The balsam fir and balsam poplar are trees that produce a healing resin. "A balm for mind and body" is the culminating definition. And the source of the word "balm" *is* "balsam."

"There is healing in old trees," Karle Wilson Baker wrote in her poem, "Let Me Grow Lovely Growing Old." "The Healing Woods" by Martha Reben is a book relating the experience of physical healing brought about by a year of remote forest living.

"My trio of poplars, with downy spring leaves delighting the eye, the pleasing penetrating scent of balm, the gay irrepressible motion of the popple bring healing," I thought as I walked on.

> Clap your hands,
> All you little poplars
> Quaking not in fear
> But in joyful praise.

Twinkling in the sunlight,
Whispering through the dark,
Flirting with the raindrops,
Twirling in the breeze.
Life may not be long,
But it can be full.
Praise the Lord!

Stately aspen,
Take your serene time
To unfold your beauty.
Your stout straight stems are
Fitting pillars for God's temple,
Draped in autumn's gold,
Summer's green canopy,
Adorned with spring's gauzy curtains,
Releasing with silken down
The seeds of eternity.
All glory to God!

O Gilead, here is your balm,
Here in the scented breeze,
Gray bark, green leaves,
Unremarkable altogether
Until that sweet incense of prayer
Is raised to the Creator.
Healing prayer,
Balm to body, mind and soul,
Pervading all of life
With a permeating fragrance
Once discovered, never lost.
Thanks be to God!

124

O worship the Creator,
You joyful leaves, you handsome leaves,
You scented leaves.
Dance my joy,
Sing my praise,
Waft my prayers of thanksgiving on perfumed air
To the throne of God,
To whom be all praise and glory!

Pine in Ordered Rows

I walked through a bed of wild strawberries as I crossed an open place to get nearer the lake. The leaves were bright red on the fall day I first noticed them. I promised myself a feast of the wild berries someday when we could be here as they ripened.

Cattails rimmed the shore and grew out into the lake here at its shallowest part. I remembered sitting in the boat at this end of the lake in late May with Fred. He fished for perch, bait for pike or food for us, depending on the size of his catch. I had absorbed the scents and sounds of spring while red-winged blackbirds swayed on old cattail stems, their cheerful "okalees" ringing over the water as they looked for nesting sites.

On foot I couldn't see much of the lake from the bank because of the cattails. I walked back through the strawberries and on to the pine plantation ahead. Here man had clearly been responsible for a drastic change in the landscape. As I approached, my first impression was of a solid mass of dark green. Closer, I distinguished individual trees, but they were all about the same height, planted in rows. There were no surprises beyond the next tree, just more pines. I usually took a good sniff of the pine scent, listened to the wind swish through the pine needles, and passed by. Individual pines growing in the open were far more interesting.

I couldn't overlook the plantation today because the trees were by far the most noticeable evidence of man's activities around our lake. In every direction except where hardwoods grow clear to the next lake north of us there are pine plantations. "We have now planted every suitable open space in the area," a ranger had told me when we met him one day inspecting seedlings in a new cutting.

Pushing through the branches that now closed the gaps between most of the maturing trees in the plantation, I was immediately in another world. The trees were many of them fifteen to twenty feet high, I guessed, looking up at the tip of new growth against the sky. They completely surrounded me. I walked on, stooping under some branches, brushing past others. I had to watch my feet. The planting furrows still persisted, making walking unpleasant and tiring. With one step up and one step down, it was as if I were walking up stairs without ever getting to the top.

The trees had been newly-planted seedlings when we built our cabin, some of them not yet poking their heads above the plowed ridges. We could see the pattern of plowed furrows plainly in the grassy meadows, and sat with our feet in them to pick the blueberries that grew so plentifully where the soil had been recently disturbed.

Now the furrows were hidden by the northern bush honeysuckles that covered the ground with first story vegetation under the pines as bracken had under the aspens. Blueberry bushes still form the ground cover in some plantations. Where growth is dense, pine needles make the only carpet. Near the highway some of the plantations have not taken hold as well and grass grows in the furrows that still receive sunlight.

Pine needles brushed my face continually, so I reached out to inspect more closely the bundles of two long needles. The two needles and the tawny bark of red pine are now firmly fixed in my mind. In contrast, white pine has five needles in a cluster.

White pine forests covered the area when lumbermen arrived here about 1880. In twenty years the pines were gone, some of them to help rebuild Chicago after the fire. The second growth which sprang up was destroyed more than once by forest fires. When most of this land became National Forest, in the 1930s, forests were replanted. Jackpine plantings are maturing along the highway, but red pine is used for reforestration around our lake. I remembered asking Ranger Pete why.

"Our soil scientist studies the carrying capacity of the soil to help us decide what species of tree to plant. Of course we consider the value and market demand of various woods, too. We are growing wood both to make a profit and to fill the needs of the consumer," Pete explained.

Arch had objected to the forestry plan. He was a hunter. "There isn't a thing in the pine plantations for the deer," he said indignantly. "All those plantations are driving the deer off to other places to look for food. They won't touch pine, and no browse of any kind grows in the plantations for them."

"We have changed our policies since these plantations were begun," Pete told me. "We employ a landscape architect now to plan our plantings as well as our cuttings. He sees that we don't plant in straight rows anymore. He works with the foresters and with our soil scientist. We leave other trees at the edges of plantations to relieve the monotonous view of pine trees. And inside the plantations we leave food trees for wildlife—beech, oak, cherry and Juneberry, for instance—as well as some for scenic purposes. We leave a few den trees, too, to shelter wildlife."

The ranger's first interest was forestry and Arch's was game. But I enjoyed scenic beauty and wanted to know more about all kinds of trees, including conifers.

Pine trees are not as "evergreen" as we think. Because the "terms of office" of their needles overlap, as Aldo Leopold explains in *Sand County Almanac*, their shedding isn't noticeable to the casual eye. The life of red needles is two and a half

128

years. White needles fall after a year and a half. I see all the conifers with new bright green needle clusters at the tips of their branches in June.

I used to call any needled tree a pine. When I found that wasn't so, I shifted to the term "evergreen." Then I met the tamaracks, or larch, in the wet places of the northwoods, and found that was wrong, too. The tamaracks turn a golden yellow in the fall, shed all their needles like deciduous trees, and grow new ones in the spring. "Conifer" is the accepted term, as the trees are all cone-bearers whether they shed their needles in turn or all at once.

One evening in mid-June these monotonous pines gave me a delightful new experience. A friend was at the cabin with me. Increasingly I found companions with whom to share the woods and increase my repertoire of seasons. As we drove through the pines, my friend rolled down the car window.

"Did you hear that?" she asked in a hushed voice. She stopped the car and turned off the motor. From far off in the distance, chiming notes of bird song floated up and up over the pine tops. Then the song started at a lower range and ascended again, each series beginning on a higher pitch.

"Let's see if we can get closer," I said. Soon the sound was all around us, echoing. "Must be hermit thrushes," I whispered. The human voice would have been a sacrilege.

> Tinkling notes shower up,
> Defying gravity and
> All earthbound senses,
> To merge into the vault
> Of the heavens,
> Reaching the very throne of God
> To return to the Creator
> My tithe of praise
> For all the melody and harmony of earth,
> For the sweetness and goodness of life.

Early ornithologists reported that the hermit thrush did not sing. They knew it only in migration, as I had at home, identifying it by its reddish-brown tail and spotted breast. It is only on its northern breeding grounds that the thrush finds its voice. Here it sings from its hidden perch in the treetops and becomes a disembodied song.

The zoom of wings as nighthawks dived for mosquitoes told us that dusk was deepening. The hermit thrush chorus was over. Across the forest came the first call of the whippoorwill. I was back to earth and to the solid facts of life.

"Do you still spray to kill the hardwoods that grow in the plantations?" I had asked the ranger. This was a sore point with me. We had witnessed the spraying of the plantation just beyond this spot, along our entrance road. The plane had flown back and forth over our heads as Fred and I sat in the boat fishing one evening. The area had a devasted look the following year with skeletons of white birch holding up ghost-like arms on the horizon.

The standing dead trunks produced excellent crops of the delicious oyster mushroom, a choice edible mushroom, in the years immediately after the spraying. The hazard in picking them was that Fred was reluctant to leave a fresh cluster, even though it seemed out of reach. I stood by calling useless warnings as he pulled himself up trunks or supported his weight on branches that cracked ominously. Luckily for my peace of mind the particular food the oyster mushrooms needed was exhausted in about three years. By the time the trees began falling the mushroom crop was gone.

"There's been no herbicide spraying—or any other kind— on the plantations anywhere in the district since 1965," Ranger Pete reassured me.

"Do you just let the hardwoods grow?" I asked.

"That would be like planting a cornfield and letting the weeds take over. No, we cut out the unwanted trees with chain saw and axe. It's much more time-consuming and expensive, but it does allow us to be selective. And we are careful that cut trees do not show above the pine, so they are not unsightly."

"I'm so glad you are not spraying. But do you mean you aren't even spraying to control insects?"

"Those of us who are responsible for both plant and animal life were concerned long before the subject of the dangers of using insecticides became popular."

"You don't spray at all?"

"Not in my district. Of course we haven't any hard-and-fast rule. If the pine plantations became badly infested with an insect pest we might consider spraying with one of the new products. There is a new insecticide whose poison disappears within three days' time, for instance."

Insects. Here was a whole part of life on earth that I had ignored, except in mosquito and blackfly time. In June the pests take over the woods. Most people just stay away, but this is one of the best times to study wildflowers and watch the forest come to life. So I have learned how to live with mosquitoes. I use the cabin door which is freest of them. I dress in the longest-legged slacks and the longest-sleeved shirts I can find.

I dislike mosquito repellent almost as much as mosquitoes. Consequently I used to go through the agony of dozens of bites stinging and itching at the same time and spend sleepless nights as a result. I reluctantly learned to cover every inch of exposed skin with the smelly liquid. It is the price of enjoying the woods in May and June.

The blackflies do not last so long, but they are sneaky little insects. They make no sound and you don't feel their bites at the time. Fred painted the boat one spring, wearing a short-sleeved shirt. Gnats kept getting in the paint. That night he was peppered with red dots. Three days later, at home, the bites swelled, festered and itched and seemed to poison his

131

whole system. He has always shrugged off mosquito bites, but since that spring he has had a healthy respect for blackflies.

There is good reason, then, to think of insects as creepy, crawly, stinging things to exterminate. You can't help noticing the ones that bite you, but of the thousand species of insects that may inhabit a backyard, only a few are harmful. Flies carry germs, mosquitoes bite, lice are unpleasant in the wrong places, and insect larvae eat vegetables and stunt flowers. But this leaves a lot of the thousand species unaccounted for.

Fireflies flash their lights charmingly, butterflies and moths are beautiful, and ladybugs are delightful. I enjoy watching dragonflies hover on their brilliant gauzy wings. Healthy soil has a large population of insects and other small living creatures, thousands to the cubic foot. They aerate the soil, cultivate it and break down the organic particles into useful soil components. Their discarded bodies become a part of its nutrients. Insects are more necessary for good soil than fertilizers. Our green world, including farm fields, would disappear without bees and other insects which pollinate the blossoms so they produce seed.

There is hardly a plant or animal, or their remains, that is not food for some insect. I remember a jingle my gardener father was fond of reciting. It went something like this:

> "Big bugs have little bugs
> Upon their backs to bite 'em.
> Little bugs have smaller bugs,
> And so—ad infinitum."

The silly little rhyme holds a basic truth about the natural world. Entomologists, the people who study "bugs," sometimes spend months and years and travel thousands of miles to study a single species. They learn about its life habits, and particularly about the species it preys upon, and the species which in turn prey upon it.

132

People have unwittingly destroyed species with pesticides and interrupted the whole chain of "bigger bugs and smaller bugs." Farmers have specialized in one crop, which encourages the insects that infest it. But this eliminates other vegetation which would harbor the natural enemies of those insects. Fighting insects with insects is a positive answer to the pesticide contamination of air, earth and water.

As I left the pine plantation, finding my way out by following a planting furrow, I wished I knew more about insects. I hoped I would not learn the hard way, by an insect infestation of these pines. That would undoubtedly mean spraying.

> Run. Run.
> Grab a spray gun.
> The insects are coming,
> Give them a squirt.
> They're gaining! They're gaining!
> Sound the alert.
> Spray 'em all dead,
> Or they'll have your shirt.
>
> Chirp, cricket.
> Crescendo, cicada.
> Bee, buzz the alarm.
> Man's on the loose!
> Fly home, ladybug,
> Pray, mantis,
> The mosquito's the villain,
> But he'll also get you!

O God, a "silent spring" would be no joke. Neither would a cornfield infested with borers or an elm tree dying of disease. Somehow, O Lord, increase our knowledge of the natural world to counteract our knowledge of deadly poisons. Our just

133

retribution is that in poisoning wildlife we also poison people. Save us, O Lord, from ourselves.

> Save me, O Lord,
>> from myself,
>> from the slow-spreading poison of doubt and uncertainty about tomorrow,
>> from the deadly mist of selfishness that blinds me to any needs but my own.
>> from the quick spurt of anger which devastates not only my life, but sprays a fog of gloom over those around me.
>> from resentment, the persistent poison whose fallout poisons my soul.

So fill me with your presence this day, omnipotent Creator, that all destructive thoughts are banished and I shall radiate only your compassion, your wisdom, your love.

Haunt Of The Duck

Sunny flowers in sunny meadows greeted me as I left the pine plantation. I was approaching the outlet stream which went through a culvert under our original entrance road. On either side of it a succession of wild flowers grew. They were not flowers you stoop to see. Most of them, in contrast to the low Canadian carpet in the forest, grow on tall stalks and flaunt their bright hues.

Fireweed caught my attention with its lovely deep rose color. I considered it plentiful in the open places of our woods until the year Fred and I drove to the cabin from Manitoba I saw acres of it sweeping whole hillsides along the Canadian highway. Fireweed flourishes in burnt over places, clothing fire-scarred landscapes in beauty.

The many buds on one spike do not open their four-petaled blossoms all at once. At the bottom, long slender seed pods are apt to curve upward, and the drooping buds at the tip to point downward. Both seem to call attention to the blossom in be-tween, and frame rather than detract from it. Fireweed often grows several feet tall and is still attractive when its seed pods turn to fluff.

Sunny yellow was the predominant color in the meadow as I walked. I had found four of the common yellow flowers that grew here listed on the same page of my flower book. The flowers grow in spikes and clusters and all except the evening primrose have five petals.

135

I appreciate the primrose best as an individual blossom. Its four large petals have a cross-shaped stigma at the center. Photographing the blossoms one day, I saw movement on a petal and realized there was a tiny spider the exact shade of the flower lurking there. A primrose-yellow spider added considerably to my new appreciation of the insect world. I discovered there is a crab spider that changes its color to match the flower it inhabits.

St. John's wort is the most plentiful of the yellow blooms. I had seen it in August with only a few blossoms open at a time, and the old brown ones persisting on ragged-looking bushes. Now I was seeing St. John's wort in its prime, forming a showy golden border along the road I walked.

Mullein spires towered over the St. John's wort but grew in much more solitary fashion. Only two or three of the tight-clustered buds open at the same time, but the single blossoms are as attractive as any garden flower. I had a new appreciation of the woolly mullein leaves when I hiked after a rain shower one day. I dug around the base of a handsome mushroom to see if the typical amanita cup was there, the poison warning. I found it, and in the process my hands acquired a coat of moist earth. I reached out and picked a mullein leaf that still had a generous amount of rain on its felt-like surface and used it as a washcloth. It worked beautifully, and I didn't have to push a button to breeze-dry my hands afterwards.

The yellow loosestrife was the fourth of the quartet. The spikes of dainty golden stars are overshadowed by showier blossoms and plants. They are also the least plentiful.

I also saw harebells, their slender leaves and stems blending with the grass so that the blue bells seemed suspended in air, bits of sky caught in grass. Several species of daisies added white blossoms to the dominant yellow. In August, fall for northwoods flowers, a parade of various asters and goldenrods would blend their lavender and gold here along the forest road.

Down among the grasses and sweet fern and blueberry bushes as I walked were the shrub-like tufts of reindeer lichen which are common in most open places around the lake. Caribou moss is another name for it. Both names indicate that it covers the tundras of the far north and furnishes food for the wildlife there. In post-glacial years caribou in this area fed upon it until they followed the glaciers on north.

The curly tufts of lichen are brittle and crunch underfoot when they are dry. When it rains the lichens become soft as a cushion and are the most comfortable and quiet to walk on of any plant I know. I would see more wildlife if I could always walk on a soft lichen cushion. The newer clusters are grayish green, but older lichens bleach to a silvery gray.

The plant is a true lichen, not a moss. Like all lichens, it is extremely durable and persistent, a combination of algae and fungi, the pioneers of the plant world. The algae and fungi team set out to "conquer the world," to "lay low the mountains," Virginia Eifert says in *Journeys in Green Places*. We have rich soil and a green world because they succeeded so well. The acids the lichens produced as they grew on bare rock crumbled it, and the long process of soil-making began. The lichens are still at it today. They grow on rocky lake shores, in wet woods, hanging from trees, clustered on logs, in dry sandy places— still busily reducing natural materials to soil.

Since lichens do not breathe as green plants do in the process of photosynthesis, they cannot rid themselves of any foreign matter they absorb. Reindeer lichen retains nearly one hundred percent of radiation particles that fall upon it and passes it along the food chain to the caribou that feed upon the lichens, to the people who feed upon the caribou. Lichens do not thrive in populated areas. They can endure all kinds of adversity except the polluted air of cities, the motor exhaust of highways. The lichens' other enemy is plenty. They cannot survive with too much food or too much water.

Adversity
Is necessity
To lowly lichen,
Fatness and plenty
Sure death.

What of me, Heavenly Father,
What of me?
Are luxury and comfort,
Ease and pleasure
Shriveling my soul?
Are the poisons of the world
Stunting my growth,
Building up in me and
Spreading to others?

But you can cleanse me, purge me,
Forgive my sins, and the whole world's.
Yes, I will confess my sins,
And I can share my plenty
With those who are in adversity,
With a cheerful heart.
I will love my neighbor.

I am not a simple lichen.
I am your child
Thank you.

I stood on the narrow culvert and traced the course of the outlet stream by the cattails that grew along and in it. The stream leaves our lake unnoticed, hidden in a cattail bed, and you have to have sharp eyes to see the tea-colored yard-wide stream flowing along beneath all the lush summer growth.

The stream flows a short distance into an overflow pond, which in turn drains into another back in the forest. In the spring, before there are leaves on trees and shrubs, you can see the stream meandering into the pond. I tried several times to walk back to it, and ended up in a wet cattail bed so thick and tall that I couldn't even glimpse the open water.

On our first trips to the cabin, Fred and I often drove at night, leaving after Sunday night meetings and arriving at breakfast time. Our headlights caught glimpses of strange ghostly objects in the undrained ditches beside Upper Michigan roads in spring.

"What are those odd things sticking up?" I asked Fred one night.

There was no other traffic, so Fred slowed to take a closer look. "Just old cattail stems," he said, stepping on the accelerator again. The tough erect stems, bleached and dead, had a whorled mass of fluff at the top where the dried seedhead had been. They were fuzzy lollipops on sticks. The flat blades of this year's new plants were not yet showing among the collapsed mass of old ones.

Now that I had done more exploring around our lake, I knew that cattails grew in every wet place. Even Cassandra Marsh has a few in the shallow water at the lake edge, mixed with shrubs. I learned they grow anywhere in the world where it is wet enough.

Cattails are so plentiful in the National Forest because the wet places have not been eliminated as they have in the agricultural areas I have lived in. Though even in farmland you can see a few cattails in a ditch and know their roots are in water. In the swamp around the Wildlife Refuge near Seney, whole fields of cattails are a common sight, stretching acre after acre.

The plants spread in two extremely efficient ways. Each brown seed spike has enough parachuted seeds in it to plant a six-acre marsh. And the starchy roots spread so fast that there can be as many as thirty-five new shoots from one plant in a season. No wonder a whole area of them can be of the same root mass. And no wonder the muskrats frequent the source of such a bountiful food supply and often live in the middle of it.

The starchy roots interested me. I told Fred flour could be

made from them, but so far he has decided it is easier to make his blueberry pancakes with flour from the grocery store. Indians didn't have grocery stores. They gathered the roots for vegetables, used the abundant pollen for special delicacies, took the long tough leaves for weaving, and lined their moccasins with the fluff from the seeds. The abundant crops reproduced themselves every year, and were not just a grocery but a whole department store!

I had always accepted the spike sticking out at the top of the sausage-shaped seedheads as part of the design. I began to appreciate the fact that nature doesn't often design without a reason. The spikes which seem so useless are the dried stalk of the pollen-producing flowers. The male and female flowers each have their own place on the stalk, instead of being combined in one blossom, or growing on two spearate plants. Without this pollen-laden tip, the seeds could not develop into the familiar brown shapes.

As I walked on, I passed a bed of coarse-lobed sensitive ferns beside the road. They are so named because the fronds wilt immediately when picked. Under them on the bare ground I once found the brown mushroom cups of *Peziza badia* growing, as large as my cupped hand.

I saw the magenta clusters of blossoms that Gladys and I had found here on our lake hike. "Swamp milkweed," Gladys had said. The sun was spotlighting them at the moment, and we both reached into our bags for our cameras.

"There you are, you handsome creature. Right where you belong," I heard my friend say. I looked around to see who or what might have joined us. Gladys was cradling a bright flower cluster in her hand.

"A friend of yours?" I asked.

"You bet. A monarch larva. Do you have something I can carry him in, along with some milkweed leaves?"

"You're going to take that creature home with you?"

140

"You've got some repulsive looking fungus in that collecting sack of yours. Guess I'm entitled to a few worms."

I laughed and handed her a paper sack. "I thought maybe those fifty Cecropia larvae in your kitchen at home were enough. I'm sure the neighbor who's feeding them for you this week thinks so. I'm terribly ignorant about moths and butterflies. Are Monarchs partial to milkweeds?" I asked, focusing my camera on a nearby blossom cluster.

"I should say they are. Monarchs are sometimes called milkweed butterflies." Several times during the week Gladys made special trips to gather milkweed leaves for the yellow-, black- and white-striped worms.

Gladys reported in a letter after she returned home: "One of the milkweed larvae died, and the second is hanging in a select place under my kitchen table. He is very slow about making his chrysalis, so I wonder if a parasite has him. The third larva is eating and growing like mad. I collected it in a different place so I have hopes for that one."

I had first become acquainted with joe-pye weed here near the outlet stream, too. I looked at the one growing in the ditch now, nearly eight feet tall. The plant sometimes grows twelve feet tall, one of my books said. "Pale pinkish purple," was the color description of the blossom in my flower book. The name, absorbed through years of reading, had always intrigued me. Now I knew the plant itself. Coarse-looking, it needs the soft lavender cluster of blossoms to redeem it.

I was delighted to find that Joe Pye was a famous Indian medicine man. He used the wild plant, along with others, and taught settlers to use it, too, as a healing herb. Joe-pye weed belongs to the large genus *Eupatorium*, plants containing oils that cause profuse sweating and are useful in reducing fevers.

Jewel weed was here also, lurking shyly beneath the bolder plants. Each tiny orange blossom hung beneath the leaves on a fragile stem, indeed a jewel. Aside from this, jewel weed has a

141

practical use. The leaves and stems, crushed and applied to the skin, are effective in counteracting the effects of poison ivy, stings and bites.

Gladys and I had decided to try to follow the outlet stream as closely as we could from the culvert to the lake, carrying our worms and mushrooms. We thrashed our way through such dense thickets of red osier and alders that I knew I had been wise to detour around it before.

"This is hiking?" Gladys asked. "Watch out! There's some poison ivy!"

I don't believe it," I said. I followed my friend's pointing finger. There it was, three shiny smooth leaves, in this dense thicket near the stream. We left quickly, working our way out to more open ground. The best prevention for poison ivy is to avoid it.

I was amazed to discover that poison ivy is a food for wildlife. A study in Indiana listed poison ivy as a preferred food for deer in that state. Our hermit thrushes eat the berries. The Illinois Department of Conservation reported that nationally more than sixty species of wildlife eat poison ivy. But human beings with any sense stay as far away from it as they can.

"What about snakes?" is one of the questions I am often asked when friends see me stretched out on the forest floor for photography.

"They say there are no poisonous species in the Upper Peninsula," I tell them. "We see small snakes occasionally, but they like warm places. In our cool woods we seldom come across them." On a warm sunny day I sometimes see a garter snake wriggling away from me in a blueberry patch or grassy meadow. I don't think I would be believed if I were to give the rest of the answer. After I have concentrated on taking a picture, I sometimes find I have been kneeling in briars, or mud and water. I could have had a snake for a companion then and never have known it.

I photographed a green-striped snake near the outlet stream one spring, coiled in the sun. I had no fear of it for myself. The snake had no more desire for my company that I for his. But I couldn't help wondering if this was an after-dinner snooze.

Black ducks nest in the thickets along the stream. I had startled one of them into flight as I crossed the culvert. There was a thrush nest a few feet from me in the fork of a many-branched alder, and in it a snake. The snake was undoubtedly there because there were eggs nearby, whether he would dine upon them now or later. Just because I personally preferred ducks and thrushes to snakes gave me no excuse for denying him his natural food.

I had walked around one of the shallow ponds on a morning when the frog population must have reached its peak. My progress was marked by a series of watery "plops." Stopping to sniff a meadowsweet spire in full bloom, I heard tiny alarmed squeaks at my feet. I took a step and looked down just in time to see a garter snake release a small frog and slither away. A tremendous leap took the frog safely into the water in an instant. I had undoubtedly saved the frog's life, but deprived the snake of a meal. Was I villain or benefactor?

> Every living creature
> Depends upon another living thing,
> Plant or animal,
> For food.
> Tomorrow the snake
> Is hunted by the owl,
> The frog dines upon a spider,
> Which in turn dines upon a fly.
> How distinguish the predator from the prey,
> The hunter from the hunted,
> The eater from the eaten,
> When the web of life

143

Is so closely meshed
That every form of life
Depends upon its relationship
With another?

Creator of the ends of the earth,
Forgive our thoughtlessness.
We deny the snake his meal
And hunt the deer for sport,
Shoot the hawk because he kills,
Then stalk his prey ourselves,
Poison harmful insects
Along with those that would control them.

You look to the whole earth
And see everything under the heavens.
You do great things which we cannot comprehend.
Whatever is under the whole heaven is yours.
Are you sure you were wise
To make us caretakers of it?

Give us wisdom,
Give us knowledge,
That we may be worthy stewards
Of life on earth,
That you may still behold
Everything you made, even man,
And find it good.

Lakeview Beach

I rested at the campsite at the east end of the lake, sitting on the bank with my feet on the sandy beach. The mouth of the outlet stream was not far away. It was good just to sit. I reached into the red hiking bag that leaned against a birch tree and unfolded my jacket. The candy bar I had tucked into the pocket would furnish much needed fuel for the rest of my jaunt.

I had taken the road that branches off just past the culvert, trying to decide whether walking was easier in the loose sand of the tracks or on the grass and vegetation between them. As usual I zig-zagged back and forth. Our first glimpse of the lake when we used the old entrance road was down this trail to the campsite. It is one of my favorite stopping places when hiking, and I had been glad to see it empty today.

Two trailers were parked here in adjoining camps over the weekend, but the area showed no signs of their occupancy. Their owners had taken good care of the forest. Off to my right I could see a camp along the lakefront. There was a cluster of tents and shelters arranged by experienced campers. They had been here when I arrived, so they were staying for their allotted two weeks.

A green canoe slid silently out from the beach near the camp and headed out into the lake. The cabin area began a short distance beyond, and the clatter of a motor suddenly disturbed natural sounds. A boat zipped out into the lake from one of the cabin docks, headed for the pike hole, and all was quiet again. The canoe swerved to avoid crossing the wake of the boat. Children came to the lakefront near the dock and splashed noisily into the water.

It was quiet the evening I had drifted here in my canoe. I was startled by a sudden clamor of wild sounds beyond the outlet stream, sounds I later described to a friend as a "bird braying."

"Oh, you must have heard a sandhill crane," Gladys laughed. "I saw an immature crane at the end of your lake one summer."

"I though they were only Seney Refuge inhabitants," I said. "Are the cranes as large as they sound?"

"Well, I have heard the greater sandhill crane called Michigan's largest and loudest bird," she said.

I was ready to believe they were loudest. After seeing three of them feeding in a field in full view from the highway one summer day on our way to town, I also accepted that they were the largest. They have long legs, a long straight neck, and a heavy body which is a uniform grayish tan. A bare red patch on the forehead is the only contrasting color.

The term "grazing," applied to their feeding, was easier to understand after I saw them, and also the word "colt" which is used for young cranes. After all, my first impulse in describing their call was to compare it to a donkey braying. Bugling and trumpeting are the words most often used to describe their cacophony of sound. The windpipe of the cranes is coiled in the breast bone like the pipes of a trumpet, making their calls so resonant they can be heard for miles.

The cranes need open places for grazing where they can probe the soil for insects, worms and grubs. Edwin Way Teale reports their favorite summer diet is blueberries and grasshoppers. But like the eagle they are tied to water habitats. The eagle needs water for his main food supply and the sandhill crane uses the shallow marshy areas for nesting and roosting. The crane, like the eagle, needs solitude, and this is the point at which they are both most vulnerable. Draining marshes for agriculture and recreational developments means death to sandhill cranes.

The greater sandhill crane population has dwindled alarmingly, even in the swampy Upper Peninsula. Maturing forests have threatened their food supply, as polluted water has the eagles'. By the simple means of coordinating wildlife and forest management, creating grassy openings near nesting sites and learning more about the crane's habits, the government has now increased the population.

We have several shallow marshy ponds near our lake. I suspected one of them might be a nesting site, after hearing about the young "colt." Fred saw a mature bird on the far side of the pond on the swamp road one day. In early spring, one of the big birds flew on seven-foot wings across a clearing in front of me as I hiked, its outstretched neck and long legs in a straight line. It was flying over this east end of the lake toward the pond. I tried to be in the right place at the right time to see more of the birds, with no luck.

One evening I decided to go for a walk to get some exercise after an inactive day at my desk. As I skirted the edge of a pine plantation, with the outlet ponds somewhere off to my right, the hermit thrush was repeating its climbing octaves of chiming notes. It was a thrush evening. I heard the song of the veery with its unmistakable hoarse descending spirals, and the more musical ascending spirals of the Swainson's thrush from the hardwoods as I left the cabin. A white-thoated sparrow piped ethereally in the distance.

It was a quiet, peaceful evening—until a male red-winged blackbird set up his shrill persistent warning notes. I knew he would not stop until I was past what he considered the danger zone around his nesting site.

Suddenly I could have sworn every instrument in a high school band began tuning up energetically at the same mo-

ment. The racket was ahead and to my left, in the pine plantation. I froze in my tracks for a stunned moment, too startled
even to reach for my binoculars. But I didn't need any magnifi-
cation to see the huge cranes that flew across the trail, below
the tree tops, off toward the ponds. Discordant crackling and
trumpeting marked their flight toward the ponds, then
stopped as abruptly as it began.

If I had not seen the birds with their huge wing span fly into
the dense second growth woods and disappear, I would not
have believed it possible. No wonder they can keep out of
sight. But what were they doing in a pine plantation? I walked
on to where the cranes had crossed the path. To my left was a
small grassy opening where planted pines had not survived. I
saw it lighted by the low evening sun—a perfect, though small,
crane grazing ground.

I wondered who had startled whom, but one thing was
certain. The cranes were as displeased as I was pleased. I
started back to the cabin, exhilarated by the experience. I had
heard and seen the sandhill cranes in their wild habitat! Afterward I realized I'd not even thought of trying to follow them to
the pond. If they were a mated pair it was possible they nested
in the marshes around the ponds. It was quite possible they
were part of a group of immature cranes using the shallow pond
for roosting at night. Like other large birds, sandhill cranes
mature slowly and spend some years in groups of their peers
before mating and nesting.

It was in thinking about the incident afterward that my
curiosity was aroused. But I was reluctant to harass the birds
whose first requirement is solitude. I would resent poeple
peering in my cabin window to observe me in my natural
habitat, too.

For a bird so sensitive to intrusion, the sandhill crane makes
a lot of noise. The trumpetings we began hearing from the
cabin of a morning filtered out some of the sounds I had heard

at close hand. We were likely hearing the cranes from the ponds as they set out for a feeding period in open uplands. We have heard them more often of recent years. The clear-cutting that I deplored creates feeding grounds for cranes as well as for deer. When Edwin and Nellie Teale visited the Seney Refuge, they saw deer and cranes grazing together.

The third large bird on our lake, the great blue heron, makes great tracks in the sand in the shallow water at the lake edge. This heron is probably the best known of large birds, as its range is practically the whole United States. We have been familiar with it since our first years on the lake when we fished the lake at dusk, as the heron did.

The large wader fishes lakes, ponds, marshes, rivers, with a long sharp beak for a spear, launching it from its coiled, elastic neck. The heron also has unlimited patience, telescopic sight and acute hearing. It can fish deeper water than most wading birds because of its long legs, and eats anything that moves in the zone.

We still see the big blue herons on our lake as frequently as we did twenty years ago. Just recently, a friend and I had arrived in early evening, at a time when all the cabins in our cove were empty. My friend, anxious to see the lake, ran down the path while I unlocked the cabin door.

"Guess what?" she said, beaming as she came back. "A blue heron was fishing at your lakefront! That's really starting our bird list in a big way!" (In Illinois, where their feeding grounds are polluted, blue herons are on the endangered list.)

Our three large birds have a comparable wing span, between six and seven feet, and are powerful in flight, but each has its own niche. The eagle needs a tall remote sparsely-branched tree for nesting, open water for fishing. The crane has to have secluded marshy areas for a nesting, open uplands for grazing. The big blue heron uses dense growths of swamp trees for its rookeries, and any kind of shallow water for fishing. The eagle and crane need solitude, but the heron is more tolerant of man's presence.

> Each in its place, Lord,
> Each in its place.
> Yellow spiders on yellow flowers,
> Monarch larvae on their milkweed food.
> Song sparrows nesting close to water,
> Woodcocks close to mud.
> Cassandra in the marshes,
> Sweet fern in the sun.
> Birches in the open,
> Beech in deepest shade.
> Deer in willow swales in summer,
> Deep in cedar swamps come winter.
> Eagles soaring in the air,
> Herons wading shallow water,
> Sandhill cranes in meadows,
> Come sundown in the marshes.

Your planning, Lord,
Is more than I can comprehend.
Why didn't you set me down and say,
"Here is your natural habitat,
Your marsh, your meadow,
Your forest, your thicket;
Here you will live and grow and die."
You could have saved you and me much trouble, Lord
But you didn't plan that way.
You gave me freedom to roam the earth,
To learn your plans for other creatures,
To comprehend their complexities,
To sample the habitats of all,
And the freedom to choose my own.
But I need your help, Lord.

You promised aid to all who call upon you.
Help me find my place on earth,
To choose my small place in the large place
You have set me.

One of the reasons I like to rest at this campsite is that I can see the whole length of the lake again. I remembered looking into a sunset from here, when the whole lake became a container which magnified the spectrum of color in massed storm clouds. Ours is a sunset lake, and this beach is the best vantage point.

I was at the narrow shallow part of the lake. I remembered the year much of the bottom of it was exposed to the sun, and bare crusty mud flats took the place of the cattail beds and reeds. The beach around the whole lake had been so wide in August that, much to our dismay, people drove cars along it. The beach became the gathering place, and we put our picnic table there rather than in the firecircle. Wild flowers grew where we usually tied the boats. Goldenrod, mint, thistles and tree seedlings sprouted on the beach like miniature forests.

That year there was not enough water to overflow into the outlet stream. I walked the whole length of the dusty stream bed, beginning here at the lake and detouring over the culvert, to the pond beyond. Water was confined to the center of the pond. All around it stretched bare expanses of dried mud, checked into irregular patches where the sun had dried and curled it. The surface seemed to support my weight, and I enjoyed the novelty of walking on the bottom of the pond without getting my feet wet.

I tested each step carefully, and when I began to feel the mud cakes quaking, I quickly retreated. I didn't want to become mired in the ooze which was beneath the sun-dried cust. Pike had certainly been banned from their natural spawning grounds that year, with no stream to take them into the pond. I retraced my steps to the lake, kicking up dust in the stream-bed.

The next spring the lake lapped at the roots of forest trees and Fred and I were again able to step directly from our boat to the bank. The cycle of lake levels had reversed. Sometimes by August we had a narrow strip of beach, sometimes not. I asked Ranger Pete for an explanation.

"Our staff hydrologist is studying the lakes. I can show you what information we have." I looked at the charts he supplied of studies of a few lakes in our area. On one page I found a comparison of graphs which answered my question. The amount of rain, the levels of well water and lake levels all dipped and rose in the same pattern.

"I can understand how rainfall affects a river which drains an area, but I can't see why it should change the level of a lake."

"It doesn't in all conditions. Soil makes the difference. These area lakes, including yours, are surrounded by porous glacial drift. Rain goes right through it and into the lake where other types of soil might hold it."

"Of course," I said. "I've seen our firecircle awash with water in a sudden shower. In an hour it's all gone. There's no way for water to drain off, it just soaks in."

"Look at this," I said, pointing excitedly to a sharp icicle dipping down on the chart in the same year for different lakes. "That's the year we built, and our lake was low, too."

I was disappointed that the year I walked the dusty bed of the outlet stream was not charted. But facts are facts. I would have to accept the unromantic obvious answer that the lake is high in years when rain is plentiful, low when it is scarce.

I took a good look around the part of the lake closest to me now. To my left were extensive cattail beds filling a large shallow bay, and beyond them the mouth of the long narrow inlet opposite the willow swales, full of bulrushes. Immediately to my left, around a point, was another reed-filled bay where the outlet stream left the lake in a bed of cattails.

To my right a peninsula of shrubs and alders formed a rounded shallow bay where I could see water lilies and picker-elweed blooming. All of this uncertain boundary line between the land and water reminded me of a conversation we had with Ranger Pete. Fred had asked why fishing in our lake was deteriorating.

"Your lake has a low carrying capacity," Ranger Pete told us.

"And what does that mean?"

"Well, there are a lot of factors involved in determining the number of fish a lake can produce, like temperature, length of seasons, other fish species in the lake, vegetation, insect life, type of lake bottom, inlets, outlets."

"So somewhere in that long list is the reason we can't catch anything but undersized pike?" Fred asked.

"There's been increased fishing, too," Ranger Pete said, gesturing to the cabins along the lake, the campers, "to clean out the big ones. Those small pike out there aren't necessarily underaged, just undersized. It is taking them longer to grow to legal size than it should."

"Should take about three years, shouldn't it?" Fred asked. "In that case, the fish released from the spawning marsh should be keepers by now."

"Our wildlife biologists have been able to produce adult northern pike from fingerlings in two years under ideal conditions, so you can see how much less than ideal your lake situation is. A good example of eutrophication."

"Of what?" Fred asked.

"In simple words, aging," the ranger said. "We are beginning to suspect that the shapes of bodies of water have a relationship to it."

This had not meant much to me at the time. Now before me was a good illustration, all these marshes along the shoreline of our lake, the many indentations, the resulting growth of vegetation. Decaying plants make soil, soil gathers around roots, and a bit more of the lake is filled in. Suddenly I realized that

Cassandra Marsh, at the farthest end of the lake from me now, was a perfect example of this process. It had once been a part of the lake and at some time far in the future would undoubtedly become forest.

I also realized that the leatherleaf grows in all the transition areas around the lake—at the changing shoreline, in boggy places in the process of becoming land. Where areas flood, the Cassandra comes in, as it had around the dead birches near my lunchstop. It grows where life is changing, and its lovely white bells silently peal out the fact that it is one of the chief agents of that change!

But the fact which hit me devastatingly as I saw it happening before my eyes was that even our lake is aging!

> Shorelines change
> With no help from man,
> Waves wash sand,
> Invade animal burrows,
> Undercut banks,
> Weaken trees
> Whose roots leave gaping holes
> And new contours.
> Reeds and cattails
> Gather sand about them,
> Decay, make soil
> For sturdier plants
> With tougher roots,
> For shrubs which vanquish lake,
> Make way for trees.
> Forest and grassland
> Are in constant competition,
> One winning, then the other,
> Even in the absence of man.
> Fire is not an invention of man,

Nor has he wholly tamed it.
Forests went up in smoke
Long before man was here to start fires,
Or to quench them.
Floods beyond our comprehension
Left rocky records of creatures
Extinct before man was here to slay them.
And lest I get too far away
In time and place,
The forest is far from stable.
Seedlings sprout, grow in competition,
Some live to make a tree,
Adding a ring to their girth,
A year to their life,
A whorl of branches to their height,
Then die in their time,
Making way for others,
Not always of their kind.
Earth is in a constant state of change.

The Deer Path

I dipped my hands in the lake to rinse the last of the chocolate from my fingers, then picked up my gear again. I was ready for the last lap of my lake jaunt. The campers had a right to privacy. I abandoned the lakefront and cut around through popple and jackpine, bracken and sweet fern, to the first cabin. From here I would follow the deer path that paralleled the lake, made long before there were human paths. The trail was a few feet back from the forest edge, giving access to the lake but providing instant cover and secrecy of movement.

I remembered again the old map of the lake that the ranger had shown me. The cabin area was a blank space on the map, marked "hardwood forest." Trees grew clear to the lakefront then, undisturbed. The only trails were made by deer and other wildlife, animals on their way to find food, to escape their enemies or to drink from the lake.

Somehow I had always thought of the service road as existing before the cabin sites were laid out. Now I saw that this road had been made for the use of summer occupants, and drastically altered the forest. Along with the eighteen cabins that had been built, with eighteen driveways leading to them, it was one of the biggest disturbances of natural features anywhere around the lake. And the powerline was there because of the cabins.

I felt a little less guilty when I remembered an aerial photo of

156

the area, taken after most of the cabins had been built. The service road did not show at all from the air, after it entered the deep forest. Some cabin clearings were dark dots in the forest roof, but I was sure none marked our cabin. Tree branches completely obscured the small opening we had made in the forest canopy when we felled the trees and set our cabin down over the stumps. Trees met over our roof and driveway.

After viewing all day what other people had done to the forest, I was forced to admit that Fred and I had benefited by the most drastic change of all. We had witnessed some of this change, since ours was only the third cabin to be built on the lake.

When our cabin was new, all the lots to the east of us were in their natural state. We felt as free to roam them as we did the surrounding forest. Of course technically, even when lots were leased, lines were thirty-five feet back from the lakefront and this area was for public use. But, as with campsites, I did not feel comfortable walking there if the cabins were occupied. I certainly wouldn't walk along picking blueberries as I used to, even though I had the right.

Cabins are used most heavily on weekends, and today most of them between the first cabin and ours were unoccupied. This meant I was free to take the deer path most of the way. For a moment, as I felt my weariness returning, I considered using the service road. At a steady pace, I could reach the cabin in five minutes. I was tempted, but I would finish what I started and amble with the deer. I likely walked the path oftener than they these days. We no longer found deer tracks on our beach as we used to do, when pine plantations had been open meadows.

One year we had found tracks leading straight through the ashes of our firecircle down the path to the lake. Now even when I am alone in the cabin, I do not look up from my desk to see deer strolling the path along the lake, as I once did. The powerline clearing where I had seen the buck at the salt lick was now perhaps the limit of their approach to the lake in the cabin area.

The first cabin sat in an open grassy area with just enough trees for shade. From this cabin to the last, there is a steady transition from open grasslands to dense forest. Here it is sunnier, drier and freer from mosquitoes. Our friends Emerson and Helen have a cabin at this end of the lake. Fred and I would come out of the woods to visit them and find them in sleeveless shirts and shorts.

There was no car at their cabin yet. We expected them any day now, and were eagerly awaiting an exchange of the year's news. Instead of hardwoods our friends have a pine plantation across the service road from them. A large white pine, matched by an equally majestic red one, marks their driveway. I walked up the path to see if everything was in order. They had added another window since I had last been here.

Trying to peer in the kitchen windows one spring to inspect our friends' newly-installed sink, I looked around for something to stand on, and saw a large morel by my foot. I picked enough mushrooms for a meal, right under their window.

"The red mushrooms are down by the lake again," Helen usually reported in August. The end of their lake path is under water in spring. The little red Hygrophorus favor the spot, and as the mushroom season accelerates in late summer it is a likely spot for other species as well. Sometimes I returned to my own cabin to find a cluster of bright-colored or oddly-shaped fungi on the step, and recognized them as Helen's calling card.

I looked toward the small knoll between our friends' cabin and the next. On its slopes I had found my first peach-colored chanterelle. The mushrooms are firm and fragrant, and the thick gills running down the stout stems have their own special beauty. Chanterelles are a favorite of French chefs. I like to prepare them because they do not lose their apricot color if cooked quickly. So many mushrooms turn dark, and though delicious don't have much eye appeal. Unlike many other mushrooms, chanterelles also grow dependably in the same place year after year. And they fruit in August when Fred and I are usually in the woods.

I attended a mushroom foray one year, a nationwide gathering of mycologists (who studied mushrooms), and mycophagists (who also ate them). When the foray ended, the cars and station wagons of the mycophagists were hung with clotheslines strung with drying chanterelles swinging gayly between back windows.

After associating with real mycologists for three days, I returned home feeling I didn't know anything about mushrooms. I would need to learn to use a microscope to make any more progress, and I was afraid I would become too fascinated with the world revealed there.

"I don't want to get lost under a microscope," I told Fred. "There's so much I want to know about trees, flowers, insects, pond life and. . . ."

"Can't you do that, too?" Fred asked.

"Remember how I have sometimes spent a whole evening trying to identify one bit of fungus? And how frustrated and unhappy I am when I don't succeed? It takes hours of painstaking work to prepare one slide, and you still have to study and compare the spores and tissue characteristics of each specimen. I'd love it, but I am afraid it would become an obsession."

Naturalist friends laughed at me. "Why did you start with mushrooms, the most difficult field of all?" they asked. They had seen what I had not at the time I was beginning nature study, that interest in one part of the natural world inevitably leads to another. I realized that I could not afford specialization. I would need another lifetime for that. I could still enjoy

159

the beauty of mushrooms, marvel at the intricate forms and numbers of species, and recognize the more familiar ones. And occasionally I might indulge in a brief mycological binge.

In tribute to this resolution, I made a detour by way of the chanterelle path as I left Helen and Emerson's cabin. There they were, colorful beauties tucked in among the glassy pipsissewa and wintergreen leaves.

As I continued on the deer path, it sometimes was so faint I had to make my own. Boats and canoes were pulled up and turned over on the bank while owners were absent, and I had to walk around them. Intersecting cabin paths were often obstacles. Some had worn down into the sand, or been cut into it, so I was forced to jump down one side and clamber up the other. Some of the cabin lakefront was in low marshing areas, but they were all small on this side of the lake. I saw several varieties of ferns including royal and cinnamon ferns as I skirted them. Here was something else to delve into someday.

When I came to an occupied cabin, I walked closer to the lake, through the blueberry bushes that covered the slopes. I had spent many happy hours picking blueberries at the lake's edge before the cabins were built. I remembered one evening in particular when there was a sandy beach and Fred was fishing on the lake. The lake was still sunny but the woods were dark as I looked up into them. I walked along, reaching out to pick berries from the bushes that hung out from the banks, spotlighted by the low sun. Without setting foot in the woods and with very little stooping, I picked enough for a pie.

More than one species of blueberry grows in our area. In the open meadows bushes are very low, seldom over a foot high, with smooth leaves. Even there a second species grows, which seems similar in every way except the berries are a dark purple instead of the usual frosty blue, and are apt to be plumper.

A taller variety with downy leaves grows in the woods and ripens later, so we can pick blueberries the whole month of

August. These bushes grow waist high and save a lot of bending.

"Those are huckleberries," more than one person has told us. And then the argument is on. Evidently any blueberry is called "huckleberry" in some part of the country. I settled the argument, in my own mind at least, with my book on Michigan shrubs. I will continue to call blue berries "blueberries," along with the black ones which grow with them on similar shrubs.

On the highest bank here is a small thicket of taller bushes which bear dark berries. The whole bush turns a beautiful maroon color in the fall. One summer when berries were scarce, neighbors insisted they were blueberries and made a pie of them for a neighborhood cookout.

We who were guests tried gallantly to keep a straight face when the first bite gave the impression a handful of sand had been added to the ingredients of the pie. Then the cook burst out laughing, and that "blueberry" pie has been better remembered than any on the lake. My shrub book said huckleberries have about ten seeds which seem to grow together. Indeed they do, and won't be separated. From then on I knew where the huckleberries grew.

I smiled as I passed the bushes now. This bank did more than grow huckleberries. Kingfishers tunnel into steep banks at the water's edge to nest. One June evening as I drifted along the shoreline in my boat, I let it crunch to a halt on the shallow sandy bottom to bird-watch. A disturbed kingfisher gave his rattling call incessantly, lighting on the tree stub from which he usually fished, flying on beyond it, then returning when I gave no sign of following.

I could see several holes in the sandy bank, and the bird's behavior confirmed my suspicion that there was a kingfisher nest here under the huckleberries. The top-heavy bluebirds use their sturdy beaks not only for fishing, but for digging the nesting tunnel after mating. They work at it from two to ten days, depending on the soil and length of the burrow, pushing the dirt out with their small feet.

While the female incubates the five to fourteen eggs, the male often busies himself digging several shorter holes nearby. So I could only guess, along with his four-footed enemies, which hole held the agitated kingfisher's progeny. I was his friend, so I pushed off and obediently followed his next flight up the lakefront.

A sandpiper skittered on the wet sand of the beach as I looked out at the lake now from the deer path. Two gulls were keeping watch, soaring over the fisherman in his boat, waiting for him to discard a mangled minnow. I came to the sunny stands of white birch, symbols of the northwoods. The glaciers had pushed birches ahead of them, down into the Middle West in their day, but as the glaciers had retreated, so had the white birch.

The gleaming white of birch bark is spectacular when one slim trunk poses against a pine. A whole forest of white birch trees is overwhelming. They gleam on the darkest rainy day, are breathtaking by moonlight. In the slanting light of late evening, they take on a golden glow.

The bark, of course, is their most outstanding feature. They are sometimes called paper birch because the outside layer peels easily and can be written upon. There is a tough orange layer beneath that is so durable Indians made canoes, baskets and many other useful items from it.

"Don't lean on that birch," I often caution hiking companions. The bark is far more lasting than the wood. I learned the hard way, taking a tumble when a decayed trunk broke with my weight. Sometimes the bark literally holds the tree up. It is common to see flattened tubes of bark on the forest floor, the wood long since decayed. I also learned not to expect a fallen birch log to hold my weight.

If any lesser authority than Rutherford Platt had reported it,

162

I might not have believed the story in his book, *American Trees*. He said that in Siberia a petrified birch log, centuries old, was found with the bark still in its natural state.

The cabin birches grow so thick and tall that most of the leaves are up against the sky, giving a misty green effect in early spring and becoming a golden crown in fall. They were too far away for me to be aware of individual leaves. Finally I searched them out and found they are oval, pointed and prominently toothed.

One spring I also became aware of the drooping tassels that hung all over a low branching birch that grew in the open. From every branch tip a cluster of pollen-producing catkins draped gracefully, swaying in the breeze, spraying a cloud of pollen. I had to look very closely to see the stiff little bottle brushes along with the budding leaves. They would later develop into seed catkins because of this pollen.

Each birch tree bears both the pollen-producing and seed-producing catkins, unlike the poplars which require a tree for each. Green catkins with scales like pine cones bear the seeds, ripening in late summer. Suddenly another mystery was solved. I had wondered about the small green scales that showered down into the firecircle and over our cabin doorstep in August. I had been too busy studying mushrooms to track them down, and besides it was difficult to study something fifty feet above my head.

It was amazing how much there was to learn about birch trees once I looked beyond the picturesque whiteness of their bark. Another characteristic which fits them for the open exposed places in which they grow is their ability to bend with the wind and storm instead of breaking. The bark is not only tough but elastic, and the wood resilient. The trees sway back and forth easily in strong winds and can bend to the ground with the weight of winter snow and ice, and spring back unharmed. A falling tree by the cabin had caught and bent a slender birch at

163

right angles. Fred removed the fallen tree, and we watched the birch day by day come slowly upright again. This trait along with its well-insulated bark fits the birch for northland winters.

The rod which seldom spared the child in pioneer days was likely to be a "birch" rod, because it is tough and elastic. The "whoosh" as it approached, and "snap" as it was applied must have been a psychological part of punishment.

"But I wonder what it did to a small boy's appreciation of birch trees," I thought. Of course, his father and mother already thought of trees and wild animals as their enemies. Nature was an adversary to be fought and conquered.

The pioneer mother in Conrad Richter's book, *The Trees*, was fearful and later despondent, because of the continuous canopy of leaves overhead. Enormous boles of ancient trees hid all sorts of fearful things, and her life, she felt, was lived in perpetual gloom and darkness because of them. Her husband measured his progress by the number of trees he fought to the death, grimly determined to hack out a clearing.

The trilogy of books Mr. Richter wrote about the family is evidence of the husband's success. The second book is called *The Farm* and the third, *The Town*. Here is the history of the country, of the change from virgin forest to farmland to urban communities. I pondered the different ways man regarded nature as his relation to it changed.

> In his brief span of life on earth
> Man has feared the natural world,
> Appeased it with offerings,
> Worshiped it.
> He has fought, conquered
> And tamed his habitat,
> Then used and manipulated it.
> Modern man ignores and belittles creation
> While destroying it,

164

Or adores and cherishes one small part
At the expense of the whole.
He is still inclined to think
The universe revolves around him.

Ruler of that universe, forgive me for thinking dominion of earth means manipulating all parts of it for my selfish use. Tilling and keeping are an expressed part of that dominion, not depleting and destroying.

With all the complexities of the natural world in balance, and my understanding of that balance, earth can yet be a friendly place to live. Nature is not my enemy, it is my very life. And so you must have meant it to be, you who created it all.

Help me to remember that you created the earth and its inhabitants before you created me, and that you looked and saw that they were good. Help me to reverence all life, even that repellent to my limited mortal perception, and to marvel at the intricacy, the precision with which one form of life fits into another and depends upon it.

Help us exercise our role of dominion, we the only creatures who have the God-given ability to comprehend and wonder at the mysteries, but who are also, because we are of the earth, inexorably linked to all its parts and subject to its law of cause and effect.

Help me, all-wise Creator, to respect the earth and understand my place in the endlessly creative chain of life.

Sunset Lake

I was almost home. Here was the path leading to our neighbor's cabin. As I crossed it and took the deer path, white pine needles brushed my face familiarly. I pushed aside branches. We would have to make a new path soon. The lakefront saplings were becoming trees. I looked up through the birch trunks to our cabin. It was snuggled down in the forest, belonging, as we did. Yes, this was home.

A sassy red squirrel scolded me from the dock trees. The small tawny animal flicked its expressive tail and watched me with bold wary eyes. This was his home too. I remembered the morning I has been wakened by unusual noises over my head. Scampering feet seemed to cover the whole roof at once. I slipped into moccasins I kept by the bed for just such occasions, and quickly stepped out the door. All was quiet. I looked up. From the peak of the roof directly above the door a small pert face looked down. I moved quietly to the side to get a better look. A red squirrel posed at the cabin peak as if it were the figurehead at the prow of a ship. Not a muscle twitched.

One small squirrel had made all that noise. I noticed the cabin roof was covered with winged maple seeds from the trees above. The squirrel must have gone wild at the bounty already gathered for him. I moved before the squirrel did, and went about my morning chores. He went back to his picnicking, his steps on the roof echoing mine on the floor below.

Beneath that floor the chipmunks were stirring, getting

ready for another day. They were usually silent down there, probably deep in their burrows. One year we heard the chattering of a family just below the floor, at the place we saw chipmunks coming and going between our foundation blocks. There was always at least one chipmunk, which we called the "housemunk," in residence. In twenty years many individuals must have had that name, for chipmunks with so many enemies live only two or three years in the wild. We learned that chipmunks appreciate their homes. Friends who live year-round in the area tried to garden. The chipmunks ate so much of it that our friends trapped the animals, marked their tails with red paint and released them at the dump about a mile away. In three hours' time the same marked chipmunks were back home in the garden.

I looked up from my typewriter one day when I heard a tapping at the cabin door. The door was open and I could see no one through the screen. The sound came again, and I saw the red head and sharp bill of a yellow-shafted flicker, pecking at the doorstep as it ate the ants there.

For several years, a shuffling sound at the door after dark announced the evening visit of a raccoon who had learned to relish the food cabin residents provided, especially bread spread with sugar and butter. He held up his front paws, with a toe missing, for any handouts, and would gladly come inside if allowed. We were all saddened one year to hear that a hunter had shot a raccoon fitting his description.

When I returned from a walk in the woods, callers had left a heap of garden vegetables on the doorstep. A peculiar knobby one had rolled away from the pile. It moved as I reached for it, and a toad hopped away under the stoop. I suspected it might have been left along with the vegetables, since neighbor children delighted in putting toads in Fred's hammock—though they claimed innocence! They insisted the toad came calling on its own.

The dead shrew we found there had not. Our grandchildren's Siamese cat brought all sorts of strange wildlife. I didn't mind the dead shrew because I was glad to have a chance to examine one. I knew the tiny voracious creatures were all about, but I had never seen more of them than a fleeting motion out of the corner of my eye. The cat's vacation hunting was over when we discovered a chipmunk tail sticking out of its mouth one day. Thereafter it was confined to the cabin.

The huge bear tracks we found in the snow had come around the corner of the cabin, to the doorstep, then to the pump. I'm glad we hadn't popped corn that evening. A friend told us of a bear that crashed through a screened cabin window for a bowl of popcorn on the table, and then left through another window when discovered.

For a while we left our garbage in a tightly closed plastic can by the doorstep. Our bed was against the same wall, and at night we'd hear a scrambling scratching sound and then the can bumping against the cabin. Skunks would worry it, jump at it till it tipped over, and roll the can halfway down the driveway trying to get at the contents.

Chipmunks, of course, are our most usual doorstep callers, since we put food for them just beyond it so we can watch them from the open door. The doorstep is their quick retreat, their vantage point as they peer from beneath. They perch on top of the stoop on a sunny day to loudly sing their praise. Their sustained chatter is subject to other interpretation by humans. Sometimes I swear they are emphatically demanding more food, letting us know the feeding station is empty of popcorn or blueberry pancakes.

I walked up the winding red-brown path to the cabin now and dumped my disorganized jumble of gear on the doorstep, while I went to the pump for a drink of cold water and splashed some on my face as well.

I opened the cabin windows wide to let in the cooling

breezes and the sounds of the forest, then threw myself down upon the couch under one of the windows to rest. I could look up and watch the tops of the forest trees sway against the sky, a soothing lullaby.

Presently I was wakened by a car door slamming, and the clank of Fred's metal tackle box and poles as he set them down. "Catch anything?" I asked as I joined him. He was pumping water into a pail and stopped to hold up a dripping fish basket. The bottom was several inches deep in small iridescent fish.

"Nice mess of bluegills," he said. "And the boys had fun. Kept me busy baiting their hooks until I made them learn to put on their own worms. I'm cleaning their fish for them, though."

Fred not only cleaned the panfish, but made a neat little filet from each side and threw the bones away. A heaping platter of the golden crisp-fried morsels was satisfying nourishment after a day spent out-of-doors.

"That's the last time I'll take a car into Blue Joe," Fred said as we lingered at the table, looking out at the woods and lake.

"Why?" I asked. The remote lake had become a symbol of bountiful fishing.

"We came very near to being stranded out there today, mired down in the ruts of the entrance road. Takes a four-wheel drive vehicle now to do it safely. If a ranger hadn't come along we might still be there."

"What about the other hundreds of lakes in the forest?" I asked hopefully.

"Can't beat Blue Joe," Fred said. "And besides, with a year's supply of fish at home in the freezer, why fish for more? Had an interesting talk with the ranger about our leases," he added.

"Oh?" I said. Maybe I would get some good news after all.

"He's as dependent on government decisions in high places as we are. But he sees the long-range policy as phasing out the summer home program."

169

The Forest Service had in fact ended the leasing of new building lots several years ago. As existing cabins had changed hands, the leases on our lake lots had all been rewritten with a common terminal date. Whether they would be renewed then or whether we'd lose our cabins would be up to the government.

I sighed. "Why don't we look for some bit of private property in the Forest, just in case?"

"With retirement so close and a home to pay for and remodel? We can't possibly take on anything else. The government will pay us a reasonable price for the building, but it wouldn't even buy a lot at today's prices."

We had worked our way through some of the practical aspects of retirement. After a good deal of looking at property we could not afford, we purchased a small rundown house on an attractive lot with trees and garden space. I had dreams of what it could become—with the expenditure of more money.

The house was in a village where Fred had once been pastor, where he could walk downtown for the morning mail, have coffee with old friends and plan the next fishing trip. A city was nearby with activities to satisfy any interest, health care facilities and, most important to me, an excellent library. But I still needed the northwoods. I like people, but I looked forward to life outside a parsonage, when I could choose my time to be with them, but also be free to plan the long hours I need to be alone for creative thought and work. The northwoods was ideal for this, as well as being my favorite subject.

"Seems to me we should be thankful for the years we've had here in the forest," Fred said.

I suddenly put my hands over my face, and shook my head from side to side. "Of course, of course," I said. 'I can't imagine what our lives would have been without this cabin. And instead of being grateful I am complaining because I want more."

Here I had been thinking about change and its inevitability all day. I had always prided myself on the way I had accepted

170

each new home, each new parish, as an adventure, looked forward to new friendships to add to the old. But I'd had the cabin. Now it was my stumbling block, the one thing I refused to give up.

"Let it go. Let it go. Let it go," I kept repeating to myself as I jumped up and began clearing the table.

The sun was low enough now to light the white birches with a golden glow. A few clouds floated in the clear sky, promising color at sunset time. The chipmunks were chirking loudly out in the sunlit woods as I wiped the table. Fred was waiting to spread out his fishing lures there so he could sort them.

Suddenly a large dark bird on silent wings swooped down through the birches and landed on the forest floor. I grabbed my binoculars from the table. Looking against the light as I was, I could see no markings, so I focussed on the head. It was a hawk of some kind, and it was striking again and again with its heavy, curved beak. All bird and animal sounds in the forest had ceased. The wings lifted and the bird flew off, navigating skillfully between the trees. I could not see what it carried. If it was one of our chipmunks, I didn't want to.

"Did you see that?" I asked Fred.

"What?" he asked, looking up from his tackle box.

"A hawk just killed something right out there outside our window. It's gone now."

I put the dishes under the sink with the breakfast ones. The lake would be beautiful for a couple of hours yet. And a Pyrawa ride was restful, called for no exertion after an active day.

As I went out the door with the foot pump for my canoe, in case it needed more air, the chipmunk chorus began again. I smiled in relief, then listened carefully. Was one voice missing? But dark wings and death are all a part of life for the small animals who nourish so many larger ones. There'd be more chipmunks. Fred had seen three young ones frolicking on the woodpile the other day as he read in the hammock.

I tucked the canoe under my arm and dropped it into the

171

water next to the fallen pine, and used the trunk for a dock. Once afloat, I rested my paddle across the boat and drifted on the quiet lake. Its surface mirrored the sunset, and I was immersed in it and all creation.

I have walked the earth today, Lord.
Thank you for going with me.
I have seen it, felt it,
Heard it, smelled it,
Tasted it.
I have been a part of the earth.

With his first squalling breath
Man breathes in air
And breathes it out, changed.
He occupies space.
With each mouthful of food
He consumes creation.
His feet make paths.

He mates and produces
More creation-users.
Those in dominion and their domain
Cannot be separated.
They were created a part of each other.

Change is the pattern
For all earthly things,
And I am of the earth.
In this sunset hour
The whole earth and sky show forth your glory.
But do I?
How can I reflect it
When my surface is ruffled
With worry about tomorrow
And the changes sure to come.

Nothing in creation is unchanging,
Yet I look for something
Permanent, solid as a rock,
Immovable, everlasting, eternal,
Dependable, adamant, unchanging,
Rooted, grounded, unshakable.
Yes. Of course.
I have just described you—the Creator!
You who laid the foundations of the earth
Are also the foundation of my life,
Yesterday, today . . . and tomorrow.

Help me fill my place
Wherever it may be
In harmony with all creation,
My fellow man—and you.

A robin sang its evensong back in the forest, sounding wild
and strange. The sun had set, color was almost gone. A bird
winged its way across the lake, silent and purposeful. There was
not enough light to see its color. The air was chill. I must go in.

I dipped my paddle in the glossy, inky water, quietly urging
the boat back toward the cabin. There was a glow over the
treetops and the round full moon floated up as I watched,
pointing a long, silvery finger toward me on the water. I
stopped paddling and sat breathless.

A door slammed back in the forest. Yes, I must go in. As
purposefully as the flying bird, I dug my paddle in the lake. The
moon disappeared behind the trees as I moved toward it. But I
wasn't ready to end this day! I turned the canoe around and
paddled back to the lakefront until the glow was bright over the
trees. I watched the moon rise again. Once more I headed for
our dock, then returned to a third moonrise. Somehow this day
was not yet complete.

Then I knew what it was. "Yes, Lord, this day *isn't* complete.

173

I relinquish Cassandra Marsh, the cabin, even the north-woods. They, too, are yours. My future is completely in your hands, even if it means losing them all. I had sought to know you better at Cassandra Marsh, and my quest has been fulfilled."

I was ready now for the day ahead and the tomorrows to come. My heart was as light as the canoe as I lifted it from the water. I tripped over Cassandra roots that were growing between the beach and the forest. I, too, was ready to accept my role in a world of change.

My feet stumbled in the dark, but I was soaring on eagle's wings . . . up . . . up . . . into bright moonlight . . . higher and surer than I had ever flown before.